Reading Connections 2

From Academic Success to Everyday Fluency

Andrew E. Bennett

ESL CENTER

HEINLE
CENGAGE Learning

Australia • Brazil • Japan • Korea • Mexico • Singapore • Spain • United Kingdom • United States

HEINLE
CENGAGE Learning

Reading Connections 2:
From Academic Success to Everyday Fluency
Andrew E. Bennett

Publisher, the Americas, Global, and Dictionaries:
Sherrise Roehr
Acquisitions Editor: Tom Jefferies
Senior Development Editor: Yeny Kim
Director of US Marketing: Jim McDonough
Senior Product Marketing Manager: Katie Kelley
Academic Marketing Manager: Caitlin Driscoll
Director of Global Marketing: Ian Martin
Director of Content and Media Production:
Michael Burggren
Senior Content Product Manager:
Maryellen E. Killeen
Senior Print Buyer: Mary Beth Hennebury

Images: All images: (c) istockphoto.com

For product information and technology assistance, contact us at
Cengage Learning Customer & Sales Support, 1-800-354-9706

For permission to use material from this text or product,
submit all requests online at **www.cengage.com/permissions**
Further permissions questions can be emailed to
permissionrequest@cengage.com

ISBN-13: 978-1-111-34862-5
ISBN-10: 1-111-34862-6

Heinle
20 Channel Center Street
Boston, MA 02210
USA

Cengage Learning is a leading provider of customized learning solutions with office locations around the globe, including Singapore, the United Kingdom, Australia, Mexico, Brazil and Japan. Locate your local office at
international.cengage.com/region

Cengage Learning products are represented in Canada by Nelson Education, Ltd.

Visit Heinle online at **elt.heinle.com**
Visit our corporate website at **www.cengage.com**

Printed in Canada
1 2 3 4 5 6 7 14 13 12 11 10

Contents

Introduction

Reading Connections 2 Overview

Reading Connections 2 combines integrated skill building and interesting content. The book contains 20 units based on a variety of modern topics. At the core of each unit is a reading passage, with interconnected vocabulary, listening, speaking, grammar, and writing activities. This comprehensive method allows students' English to rapidly improve. At the same time, engaging topics keep students interested and motivated while they learn.

Following are the features found in each unit of *Reading Connections 2*.

Pre-Reading Questions

This exercise includes three simple questions about the topic. It's designed to get students to start thinking about the topic for a few minutes. The exercise can be done in pairs, or the entire class can discuss the questions together.

Consider the Topic

This pre-reading exercise gives each student a chance to register his or her opinion about three statements related to the topic. The exercise helps make students more active and interested learners.

Reading Passage

The core component of each unit is an article about a modern topic. The topics are from a wide range of fields, including technology, health, science, modern lifestyles, sports, the environment, and more. This variety reflects the wide range of our daily literacy experiences and the breadth of issues facing us in the 21st century.

Each article in *Reading Connections 2* is about 300 words long. The vocabulary and grammar are carefully controlled, to improve comprehension and allow for focused instruction. The unit's target vocabulary words and phrases (which are tested in the Vocabulary Building and Phrase Building exercises) are bolded for easy reference.

Above the article is an audio CD icon. Next to it is a track number, indicating the track on the audio CD where students can listen to a recording of the article. Beneath the article is a glossary with definitions of the article's challenging words and phrases. The definitions are written in simplified English.

Questions about the Reading

There are five multiple choice comprehension questions. A wide variety of question types are used, including main idea, detail, vocabulary in context, and more.

Writing about the Article

This exercise gives students a chance to write short responses to questions about the article. To make things easier, the first few words of each answer are given. Each answer should be one sentence long.

Vocabulary Building

In this exercise, the unit's eight target vocabulary words are tested. The target words were selected for their usefulness and frequency of use. They are the words students are going to use and encounter over and over when speaking, reading, and writing English.

Phrase Building

This exercise tests the unit's three target phrases. It is in a "cloze passage" format. Phrases should be used only once, and students should make sure to use the correct word form. Note that there are four phrases but only three blanks. The extra phrase is there to reduce the impact of guessing.

Grammar Exercise

This exercise focuses on important grammar skills. It is designed to strengthen students' proficiency in reading and writing key language structures. Each exercise is based on a structure found in the unit's Reading Passage.

Listening Exercise

The three questions in this exercise are based on a short conversation (about 60 words long) between two people. The conversation, which is recorded on the audio CD, is related to the unit's topic. (The track number is written next to the audio CD icon.) Not only is this exercise good practice for strengthening general listening skills, but it's also excellent practice for tests such as TOEIC and TOEFL.

Listening Activity

This activity is based on a short talk (about 60 words long). Each talk, which is related to the unit's topic, is recorded on the audio CD. (The track number is written next to the audio CD icon.) A variety of talk types are used, including information announcements, advertisements, introductions, and others. This activity gives students practice listening for key details, just as they would in the real world.

Discussion Questions

Now it's time for students to discuss questions related to the unit's topic. As they've already read an article and listened to a conversation and short talk about the topic (in addition to doing many other exercises), it's time for students to share their own ideas. The three questions in this exercise can be discussed in pairs, or the class can discuss the questions together.

Discussion Activity

This is the final exercise in each unit. Groups of classmates work together on a discussion activity. Simple directions for the activity are given, and a model example is provided to help students start talking.

ESL CENTEP

Reading Connections Program Overview

Reading Connections is a NEW five-level series designed to develop the language and fluency necessary for success in real world and academic settings. The following pages highlight and explain key features of the *Reading Connections* program.

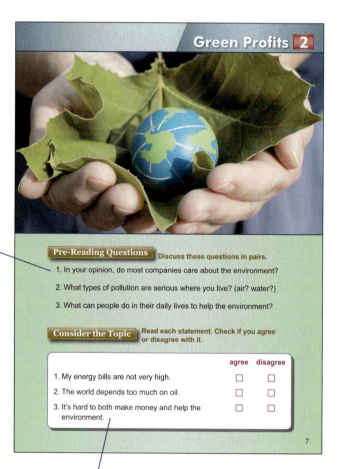

Pre-Reading questions designed for pair, group, or class discussion introduce the unit topic for increased comprehension of the reading to follow.

Consider the Topic sections give students the opportunity to create valuable connections between the reading topic and their own lives.

Unique and engaging readings, including contemporary topics such as **viral marketing** and **YouTube**, connect academic content to real world fluency.

Questions about the Reading sections in every unit assess student comprehension of the passage while teaching valuable reading skills such as finding the main idea, looking for detail, learning vocabulary in context, and making inferences. Perfect for **critical thinking** practice!

Unit 2

Green Profits

Reading Passage 🔘 Track 4

1   In the past, few companies tried to be friends of the **environment**. They **generally** felt that saving the world meant losing money. These days, companies face a lot of pressure to "go green." At the same time, they're learning that helping the world can lead to healthy profits.

5   The pressure on companies to go green comes from several areas. First, energy prices are rising **all the time**. That has led to a big **demand** for products that use less energy. Second, many governments are making companies lower their pollution levels. That has helped **speed** the growth of "clean" technologies. Third, **consumers** are paying more attention to issues like global warming.
10 As a recent study showed, 66% of people **prefer** to buy from environmentally friendly companies.

   Transportation is one industry going through big changes. With **oil** prices higher than ever, hybrid cars have become very popular. Toyota, a leader in the field, has already sold more than one million hybrids. By 2015, hybrids could
15 make up 30% of all car sales. That would make the segment worth $1 trillion.

   Energy companies are also changing. GE, a major US firm, has lowered the energy needs of its light bulbs, refrigerators, and other products. While improving its image, the company is attracting consumers who want to lower their bills. Also, energy suppliers like England's BP are slowly **moving away**
20 **from** dirty energy sources like oil. In 2005, BP's sales for solar energy were $350 million. In 2008, the company's sales **target** for solar energy rose to $1 billion.

   A whole host of other industries, from real estate to food packaging, are going green. And, they're doing so while earning money.
25 That's very important to company owners and shareholders. When targets for higher profits and lower pollution can both be met, it's a win-win situation.

¹³ hybrid cars – cars that run on gas and electricity
¹⁵ segment – part/section
²⁰ solar – from the sun
²² real estate – houses and other buildings
²⁶ shareholder – person who owns part of a company

8

Questions about the Reading   Choose the best answer.

1. (   ) What is the main idea?
     (A) Companies can make money while helping the Earth.
     (B) Governments put too much pressure on companies.
     (C) People care about profits more than anything else.
     (D) Solar energy will soon replace dirty energy sources.

2. (   ) What does the article suggest about clean technologies?
     (A) They may not be worth the high cost.
     (B) They are used by every company.
     (C) They help lower pollution levels.
     (D) They lead to higher energy prices.

3. (   ) How much did one company bring in from solar energy in 2005?
     (A) $30 million
     (B) $350 million
     (C) $1 billion
     (D) $1 trillion

4. (   ) What does the phrase *go green* in line 3 mean?
     (A) Find a way to make more money
     (B) Start caring for the environment
     (C) Give away part of one's profits
     (D) Earn as much money as possible

5. (   ) Why does the article mention GE's new refrigerators?
     (A) To give an example of a product that uses less energy
     (B) To offer a reason why consumers can't pay their bills
     (C) To explain how all companies waste too much energy
     (D) To suggest that people should use refrigerators less often

Writing about the Article   Answer each question based on the article.

1. What are governments making companies do?
     They are making companies   .

2. How much might the hybrid car market be worth in 2015?
     By 2015, it   .

3. What are some GE products with lower energy needs?
     Two examples are   .

9

Writing about the Article activities ask students to write short answers in complete sentences, assessing reading comprehension while practicing writing skills.

Vocabulary Building exercises test the unit's target vocabulary in exercises designed both to assess comprehension and apply high-frequency terms to meaningful contexts.

Grammar Exercise sections provide practice in a target grammatical structure introduced in the reading passage to enhance overall comprehension and provide students with the skills necessary to read, write, and speak appropriately.

Unit 2

Green Profits

Vocabulary Building — Choose the best word to fill in each blank.

1. My _____ this year is to sell 100 houses.
   (A) level   (B) product   (C) target   (D) source

2. The used _____ from the factory is black and dirty. We always recycle it.
   (A) oil   (B) technology   (C) energy   (D) money

3. Do you _____ living in big cities or small towns? Personally, I like cities.
   (A) feel   (B) become   (C) face   (D) prefer

4. _____ are looking for high quality gifts at low prices.
   (A) Consumers   (B) Fields   (C) Industries   (D) Companies

5. _____, I don't eat big meals, but today is a holiday!
   (A) Even   (B) Generally   (C) Already   (D) Slowly

6. Opening offices abroad can _____ our growth in other countries.
   (A) attract   (B) lower   (C) speed   (D) sell

7. I ride my bicycle to work and around town. It keeps me healthy, and it's good for the _____.
   (A) field   (B) situation   (C) pollution   (D) environment

8. I want to open a coffee shop. In this area, there's a big _____ for places to sit and talk.
   (A) leader   (B) demand   (C) study   (D) product

Phrase Building — Write the correct phrase in each blank.

● move away from   ● a whole host of   ● make up   ● all the time

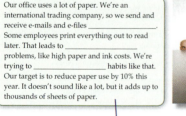

Our office uses a lot of paper. We're an international trading company, so we send and receive e-mails and e-files _____. Some employees print everything out to read later. That leads to _____ problems, like high paper and ink costs. We're trying to _____ habits like that. Our target is to reduce paper use by 10% this year. It doesn't sound like a lot, but it adds up to thousands of sheets of paper.

Grammar Exercise

Adverb Clauses

Fill in each blank with *while*, *although*, **or** *because*.

Example: _____ I'm full, I'll join you for an ice cream.
Answer: *Although* I'm full, I'll join you for an ice cream.

1. We canceled the trip _____ too few people signed up.

2. _____ I look for Tim, why don't you get the car started.

3. _____ tickets are expensive, I still want to go to the concert.

4. _____ it was raining, Mary decided to go out for a walk.

5. People complained about the waiter _____ he was slow and careless.

Listening Exercise — Track 5

Listen to the conversation. Then, answer the following questions.

1. ( ) What did Union Tinworks do?
   (A) They lowered their pollution output.
   (B) They raised their earnings target.
   (C) They cleaned up a nearby river.
   (D) They changed their product line.

2. ( ) How did the company get into trouble in the past?
   (A) By polluting a river
   (B) By lying to the government
   (C) By changing their image
   (D) By wasting money

3. ( ) How much was the company fined?
   (A) $2,500
   (B) $5,000
   (C) $25,000
   (D) $50,000

Phrase Building activities assess and apply the unit's target phrases in a cloze exercise.

Listening Exercises in every unit offer thematically-related conversations in MP3 format on audio CD or online that assess student comprehension for test-preparation and for building fluency.

Listening Activity sections prompt students to listen and record key details from a short talk offered in a variety of formats such as advertisements and introductions to build real-world fluency.

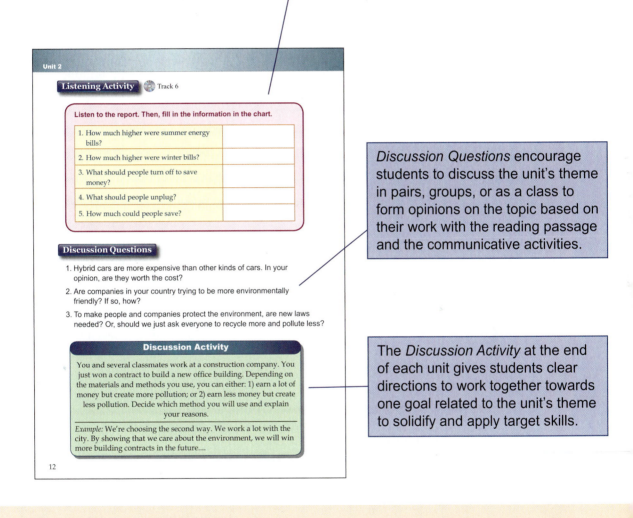

Unit 2

Listening Activity Track 6

Listen to the report. Then, fill in the information in the chart.

1. How much higher were summer energy bills?	
2. How much higher were winter bills?	
3. What should people turn off to save money?	
4. What should people unplug?	
5. How much could people save?	

Discussion Questions

1. Hybrid cars are more expensive than other kinds of cars. In your opinion, are they worth the cost?

2. Are companies in your country trying to be more environmentally friendly? If so, how?

3. To make people and companies protect the environment, are new laws needed? Or, should we just ask everyone to recycle more and pollute less?

Discussion Activity

You and several classmates work at a construction company. You just won a contract to build a new office building. Depending on the materials and methods you use, you can either: 1) earn a lot of money but create more pollution; or 2) earn less money but create less pollution. Decide which method you will use and explain your reasons.

Example: We're choosing the second way. We work a lot with the city. By showing that we care about the environment, we will win more building contracts in the future....

12

Discussion Questions encourage students to discuss the unit's theme in pairs, groups, or as a class to form opinions on the topic based on their work with the reading passage and the communicative activities.

The *Discussion Activity* at the end of each unit gives students clear directions to work together towards one goal related to the unit's theme to solidify and apply target skills.

Audio recordings of all student book readings available in MP3 files on audio CD and FREE online at elt.heinle.com/readingconnections

Also **available**:

Assessment CD-ROM with Exam*View*® allows teachers to create tests and quizzes quickly easily!

Scope and Sequence

	Theme	Reading Skills	Grammar	Listening Exercise & Activity	Discussion Activity
1	Education	Identifying details; using vocabulary in context	Gerunds vs. Infinitives	Conversation about a new kind of computer; report about the XO computer	Planning a non-profit organization
2	Business and the Environment	Identifying the main idea and details; using vocabulary in context; recognizing suggestions	Adverb Clauses	Conversation about a polluting company; report about energy costs	Planning a new office building
3	Animals	Identifying the main idea and details; using vocabulary in context; recognizing suggestions	Adjectives + Prepositions	Conversation about finding boarding for a pet; report about a singing dog	Designing a pet hotel
4	Fashion	Identifying details; using vocabulary in context; recognizing suggestions	Elsewhere, Everywhere, and Nowhere	Conversation about designer clothing; report about a major fashion label	Designing an item of clothing
5	The Internet	Identifying the main idea and details; recognizing suggestions	Prepositions of Place	Conversation about an advertisement; report about a viral marketing campaign	Planning a viral marketing campaign
6	Sports	Identifying the main idea and details	Verb Form	Conversation about a sporting event; report about a basketball game	Promoting sports from one's home country

	Theme	Reading Skills	Grammar	Listening Exercise & Activity	Discussion Activity
7	The Media	Identifying the main idea and details; recognizing suggestions	However, Wherever, and Whatever	Conversation about a celebrity; report about a band making a comeback	Inventing a gossip story about a celebrity
8	Careers	Identifying details; using vocabulary in context; recognizing suggestions	Pronouns	Conversation about a T-shirt business; ad for a course about running a SOHO	Planning a three-person SOHO
9	The Environment	Identifying the main idea and details; using vocabulary in context	Other and Another	Conversation about forests; report about a tree planting event	Planning a club to help the environment
10	Culture	Identifying details; recognizing suggestions	Since, For, and Until	Conversation about special tea drinks; report about milk tea	Planning a day trip for a foreign guest
11	Charity	Identifying the main topic and details; recognizing implications	Adjective Clauses	Conversation about a lottery winner; report about a charity auction	Discussing how to donate money
12	The Arts	Identifying the main idea and details; using vocabulary in context	The Passive Voice	Conversation about a computer actor; report about a group of actors	Holding a mini debate about computer graphics in movies

	Theme	Reading Skills	Grammar	Listening Exercise & Activity	Discussion Activity
13	World Cities	Identifying details; understanding purpose	Quantifiers	Conversation about traveling in New York; report about events in New York	Planning two days of cultural events
14	21st Century Challenges	Identifying the main idea and details; recognizing suggestions	Word Form	Conversation about a water shortage; report about a polluted river	Coming up with plans to deal with a water shortage
15	Culture	Identifying the main idea and details; using vocabulary in context; recognizing implications	Every, Any, and All	Conversation about a French movie; report about a culture fair	Making an ad for a cultural product
16	Growing and Aging	Identifying details; recognizing suggestions	To, For, and With	Conversation about a career in healthcare; report about the average retirement age	Making a plan to deal with an aging population
17	The Internet	Identifying the main idea and details; using vocabulary in context	Noun Clauses	Conversation about a funny video; report about using video in a marketing campaign	Holding a YouTube style mini debate
18	Social Issues	Identifying the main idea and details	Adjectives vs. Adverbs	Conversation about a problem with credit cards; report about overcoming credit problems	Debating the pros and cons of credit cards

	Theme	Reading Skills	Grammar	Listening Exercise & Activity	Discussion Activity
19	Health	Identifying details; using vocabulary in context	Singular vs. Plural	Conversation about a yoga class; advertisement for a yoga school	Developing a plan for getting into better shape
20	Science and Technology	Identifying the main idea and details; recognizing suggestions	Be, Been, and Being	Conversation about DNA and a criminal case; report about DNA evidence	Talking about crime scene evidence

Discuss these questions in pairs.

1. In your country, how old are children when they start using computers?

2. How can computers be used in a classroom?

3. Would children in poor countries benefit from having laptop computers? If so, how?

Consider the Topic **Read each statement. Check if you agree or disagree with it.**

	agree	disagree
1. Computers are an important educational tool.	☐	☐
2. In poor countries, few parents can afford to buy computers for their children.	☐	☐
3. Children in poor countries have easy lives.	☐	☐

Reading Passage 🔘 Track 1

1   In many poor countries, children receive a low standard of education.
     Classrooms have few supplies, teaching materials, and books. One **non-profit**
     group trying to change that is the One Laptop per Child (OLPC) foundation.
     Its goal is to provide the world's children with cheap, but **powerful** notebook
5   computers.

     OLPC was founded in 2005 by Nicholas Negroponte, a computer expert at
     MIT. His ideas received support from computer companies, the UN, and
     government **leaders**. The group's original goal was to sell the computers for
     $100 each. However, the actual price of the first XO model laptops **turned out**
10   to be $188.

     The XO is special **in that** it is a children's notebook. The keyboard is small and
     waterproof, and the machine is built to **withstand** being dropped. The XO also
     has a webcam (which children love) for taking pictures and recording videos.
     There's also built-in Wi-Fi to make it easy to connect to the Internet.

15   In the classroom, the XO has many **functions**. It can be used to take notes and
     do homework. Plus, students can draw pictures and create reports. The XO is
     also an e-book reader, and it comes with many books pre-installed. In fact, one
     of the **device's** goals is to replace books in schools with limited resources.

     The XO **went into production** in November
20   2007. Teachers in places like Peru and Nigeria are
     already reporting a difference. They say children
     are more excited about learning. Young **scholars**
     are also making new friends in other countries via
     the Internet. Children are even using the XO to
25   teach their parents at home.

     Many experts see technology as a way for the world's poor to improve their
     lives. OLPC's mission statement talks about bringing the "light of learning"
     into children's lives. Indeed, with tools like the XO in their hands, children are
     given a sense of hope for a brighter future.

---

³ foundation – group; organization   ¹⁴ Wi-Fi – wireless Internet connection
⁹ actual – real   ²⁷ mission – goal

Questions about the Reading — Choose the best answer.

1. (   ) What does the OLPC foundation want to do?
  (A) Lower the price of computers worldwide
  (B) Sell inexpensive books to poor students
  (C) Supply students with low-priced computers
  (D) Give money to poor students for computers

2. (   ) Which of these benefits of the XO is NOT mentioned in the article?
  (A) Its keyboard is a good size for kids.
  (B) Part of it is waterproof.
  (C) It is strong and durable.
  (D) The machine is very light.

3. (   ) Why does the article mention an "e-book reader"?
  (A) To suggest how the XO may replace books
  (B) To give an example of a product complaint
  (C) To introduce the XO's production schedule
  (D) To support the idea that the XO is cheap

4. (   ) What does the word *brighter* in line 29 mean?
  (A) shinier
  (B) better
  (C) smarter
  (D) clearer

5. (   ) How is the XO already making a difference in children's lives?
  (A) It's leading to higher test scores.
  (B) It's helping children make new friends.
  (C) It's making it possible for children to work after school.
  (D) It's providing a way for their parents to go back to school.

Writing about the Article — Answer each question based on the article.

1. Who has supported Mr. Negroponte?
  He has received support _____ .

2. What allows the XO to connect to the Internet?
  The XO has _____ .

3. Where has the XO already been used by students?
  The XO has been used _____ .

Vocabulary Building
Choose the best word to fill in each blank.

1. A thermometer is a _____ that is used to measure the temperature.
   (A) function   (B) device   (C) power   (D) scholar

2. Because my jacket is _____, I kept dry during the storm.
   (A) non-profit   (B) original   (C) waterproof   (D) excited

3. Desert plants can _____ high temperatures and need little water.
   (A) withstand   (B) lead   (C) limit   (D) record

4. In school, the teacher is the _____ of the classroom.
   (A) mission   (B) standard   (C) idea   (D) leader

5. Making money is not the goal of a(n) _____ organization.
   (A) non-profit   (B) functional   (C) actual   (D) small

6. The _____ typhoon damaged many buildings along the coast.
   (A) hopeful   (B) powerful   (C) original   (D) leading

7. The _____ of my cell phone include making calls, text messaging, and taking photographs.
   (A) experts   (B) machines   (C) functions   (D) devices

8. Alex is an excellent _____. He loves to study and does very well in school.
   (A) group   (B) scholar   (C) statement   (D) report

Phrase Building
Write the correct phrase in each blank. (Remember to use the correct word form.)

● go into production   ● in that   ● turn out   ● take notes

ELECTRIC
VEHICLE
CHARGING
STATION

The Tesla Roadster is a very special car, _____ it does not use gasoline. Instead, it runs on electricity. The car first _____ in 2008. People used to worry that no one would want to drive an electric car. As it _____, the Tesla Roadster is very popular. In fact, the company cannot make the cars quickly enough. After ordering a Roadster, people have to wait months before receiving it.

Grammar Exercise

Gerunds vs. Infinitives

Circle the correct form of the word.

Example: This device is used (to measure/measuring) wind speed.
Answer: This device is used *to measure* wind speed.

1. Tomorrow, she plans (to visit/visiting) the science museum.

2. I usually use this camera (to take/taking) indoor photos.

3. The MP3 player comes with a cable for (to transfer/transferring) files to and from your computer.

4. If you have any trouble (to set/setting) up your website, just let me know.

5. The sky is turning dark, so you might want (to bring/bringing) an umbrella.

Listening Exercise ⊙ Track 2

Listen to the conversation. Then, answer the following questions.

1. (   ) What did the man do last night?
   (A) He bought a computer.
   (B) He watched a TV show.
   (C) He did his schoolwork.
   (D) He surfed the Internet.

2. (   ) How did the woman learn about the XO?
   (A) She read a news article about it.
   (B) She saw a TV program about it.
   (C) A friend told her about it.
   (D) She learned about it in class.

3. (   ) What is the man's opinion of the XO?
   (A) He thinks the XO is poorly made.
   (B) He believes it's an excellent idea.
   (C) He feels the machine is too expensive.
   (D) He's worried it may be misused.

Listening Activity Track 3

Listen to the report. Then, fill in the information in the chart.

1. Aside from the battery, how does the speaker describe the XO's technology?	
2. How long can you surf the Internet with the XO?	
3. How long can you read e-books with the XO?	
4. How many times can you recharge the XO?	
5. How many times can you recharge a regular laptop?	

Discussion Questions

1. In what ways can the Internet be used for educational purposes?

2. The XO was designed with poor children in mind. However, do you think children in every country (including rich countries) would benefit from having a machine like the XO?

3. In your opinion, will most students use the XO for learning? Or, will they just play games and have fun with it?

Discussion Activity

Plan a non-profit organization. First, decide what type of organization you will create. Then, figure out a way to raise money. For example, will you sell something? Will you ask the government for help?

Example: We're going to start a hurricane relief organization. We will send medical supplies to people who need them. We might have to ask the government for help....

Pre-Reading Questions Discuss these questions in pairs.

1. In your opinion, do most companies care about the environment?

2. What types of pollution are serious where you live? (air? water?)

3. What can people do in their daily lives to help the environment?

Consider the Topic Read each statement. Check if you agree or disagree with it.

	agree	disagree
1. My energy bills are not very high.	☐	☐
2. The world depends too much on oil.	☐	☐
3. It's hard to both make money and help the environment.	☐	☐

Reading Passage 🔘 Track 4

1   In the past, few companies tried to be friends of the **environment**. They **generally** felt that saving the world meant losing money. These days, companies face a lot of pressure to "go green." At the same time, they're learning that helping the world can lead to healthy profits.

5   The pressure on companies to go green comes from several areas. First, energy prices are rising **all the time**. That has led to a big **demand** for products that use less energy. Second, many governments are making companies lower their pollution levels. That has helped **speed** the growth of "clean" technologies. Third, **consumers** are paying more attention to issues like global warming.

10 As a recent study showed, 66% of people **prefer** to buy from environmentally friendly companies.

Transportation is one industry going through big changes. With **oil** prices higher than ever, hybrid cars have become very popular. Toyota, a leader in the field, has already sold more than one million hybrids. By 2015, hybrids could

15 make up 30% of all car sales. That would make the segment worth $1 trillion.

Energy companies are also changing. GE, a major US firm, has lowered the energy needs of its light bulbs, refrigerators, and other products. While improving its image, the company is attracting consumers who want to lower their bills. Also, energy suppliers like England's BP are slowly **moving away**

20 **from** dirty energy sources like oil. In 2005, BP's sales for solar energy were $350 million. In 2008, the company's sales **target** for solar energy rose to $1 billion.

A whole host of other industries, from real estate to food packaging, are going green. And, they're doing so while earning money.

25 That's very important to company owners and shareholders. When targets for higher profits and lower pollution can both be met, it's a win-win situation.

---

¹³ hybrid cars – cars that run on gas and electricity
¹⁵ segment – part/section
²⁰ solar – from the sun
²² real estate – houses and other buildings
²⁶ shareholder – person who owns part of a company

Questions about the Reading

1. (   ) What is the main idea?
  - (A) Companies can make money while helping the Earth.
  - (B) Governments put too much pressure on companies.
  - (C) People care about profits more than anything else.
  - (D) Solar energy will soon replace dirty energy sources.

2. (   ) What does the article suggest about clean technologies?
  - (A) They may not be worth the high cost.
  - (B) They are used by every company.
  - (C) They help lower pollution levels.
  - (D) They lead to higher energy prices.

3. (   ) How much did one company bring in from solar energy in 2005?
  - (A) $30 million
  - (B) $350 million
  - (C) $1 billion
  - (D) $1 trillion

4. (   ) What does the phrase *go green* in line 3 mean?
  - (A) Find a way to make more money
  - (B) Start caring for the environment
  - (C) Give away part of one's profits
  - (D) Earn as much money as possible

5. (   ) Why does the article mention GE's new refrigerators?
  - (A) To give an example of a product that uses less energy
  - (B) To offer a reason why consumers can't pay their bills
  - (C) To explain how all companies waste too much energy
  - (D) To suggest that people should use refrigerators less often

Writing about the Article

1. What are governments making companies do?

   They are making companies _____ .

2. How much might the hybrid car market be worth in 2015?

   By 2015, it _____ .

3. What are some GE products with lower energy needs?

   Two examples are _____ .

Vocabulary Building — Choose the best word to fill in each blank.

1. My _____ this year is to sell 100 houses.
   (A) level   (B) product   (C) target   (D) source

2. The used _____ from the factory is black and dirty. We always recycle it.
   (A) oil   (B) technology   (C) energy   (D) money

3. Do you _____ living in big cities or small towns? Personally, I like cities.
   (A) feel   (B) become   (C) face   (D) prefer

4. _____ are looking for high quality gifts at low prices.
   (A) Consumers (B) Fields   (C) Industries   (D) Companies

5. _____, I don't eat big meals, but today is a holiday!
   (A) Even   (B) Generally   (C) Already   (D) Slowly

6. Opening offices abroad can _____ our growth in other countries.
   (A) attract   (B) lower   (C) speed   (D) sell

7. I ride my bicycle to work and around town. It keeps me healthy, and it's good for the _____.
   (A) field   (B) situation   (C) pollution   (D) environment

8. I want to open a coffee shop. In this area, there's a big _____ for places to sit and talk.
   (A) leader   (B) demand   (C) study   (D) product

Phrase Building — Write the correct phrase in each blank.

● move away from   ● a whole host of   ● make up   ● all the time

Our office uses a lot of paper. We're an international trading company, so we send and receive e-mails and e-files _____. Some employees print everything out to read later. That leads to _____ problems, like high paper and ink costs. We're trying to _____ habits like that. Our target is to reduce paper use by 10% this year. It doesn't sound like a lot, but it adds up to thousands of sheets of paper.

Grammar Exercise

Adverb Clauses

Fill in each blank with *while*, *although*, **or** *because*.

Example: _____ I'm full, I'll join you for an ice cream.
Answer: *Although* I'm full, I'll join you for an ice cream.

1. We canceled the trip _____ too few people signed up.

2. _____ I look for Tim, why don't you get the car started.

3. _____ tickets are expensive, I still want to go to the concert.

4. _____ it was raining, Mary decided to go out for a walk.

5. People complained about the waiter _____ he was slow and careless.

Listening Exercise Track 5

Listen to the conversation. Then, answer the following questions.

1. (   ) What did Union Tinworks do?
   (A) They lowered their pollution output.
   (B) They raised their earnings target.
   (C) They cleaned up a nearby river.
   (D) They changed their product line.

2. (   ) How did the company get into trouble in the past?
   (A) By polluting a river
   (B) By lying to the government
   (C) By changing their image
   (D) By wasting money

3. (   ) How much was the company fined?
   (A) $2,500
   (B) $5,000
   (C) $25,000
   (D) $50,000

Listening Activity Track 6

Listen to the report. Then, fill in the information in the chart.

1. How much higher were summer energy bills?	
2. How much higher were winter bills?	
3. What should people turn off to save money?	
4. What should people unplug?	
5. How much could people save?	

Discussion Questions

1. Hybrid cars are more expensive than other kinds of cars. In your opinion, are they worth the cost?

2. Are companies in your country trying to be more environmentally friendly? If so, how?

3. To make people and companies protect the environment, are new laws needed? Or, should we just ask everyone to recycle more and pollute less?

Discussion Activity

You and several classmates work at a construction company. You just won a contract to build a new office building. Depending on the materials and methods you use, you can either: 1) earn a lot of money but create more pollution; or 2) earn less money but create less pollution. Decide which method you will use and explain your reasons.

Example: We're choosing the second way. We work a lot with the city. By showing that we care about the environment, we will win more building contracts in the future....

Pre-Reading Questions

Discuss these questions in pairs.

1. Do you have any pets?

2. What do you think about animals wearing clothes?

3. Would you ever take a pet on vacation?

Consider the Topic

Read each statement. Check if you agree or disagree with it.

	agree	disagree
1. Pets make very good friends.	☐	☐
2. It's expensive to raise an animal.	☐	☐
3. We should treat pets as well as our children.	☐	☐

Reading Passage 💿 Track 7

1 Don't tell Cindy Hamilton that her poodle Marcy is just a dog. As Cindy will quickly tell you, Marcy is a full member of the family. Dressed in style, she goes everywhere with the family. Indeed, from designer clothes to **luxury** hotels, **pets** can have it all these days. It's not a bad time to be a furry friend.

5 In many countries, it's common to see people **out on the town** with their pets. Sometimes, animals are dressed better than their masters. Thanks to a booming pet wear industry, your dog, cat, mouse, or bird has more fashion choices than ever. Store shelves are filled with **fancy** coats, shoes, dresses, and collars.

10 To help a pet look his or her best, grooming services can give your little buddy a **gorgeous** haircut. After spending an afternoon at a pet spa, why not go out for **a bite to eat**? Some restaurants welcome pets. They **provide** water and treats for your companion. Some even have special menus so you can order something to eat for your dog!

15 Families going on vacation no longer have to worry about leaving their pets at home. Pet hotels can watch your animal for you. Some, like The Barkley in Ohio, USA, offer a range of cage types. The best cages even come with a TV that shows animal programs.

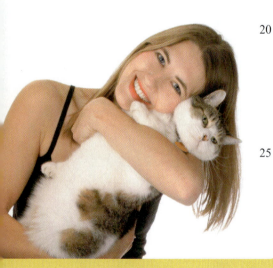

For those who **can't bear to** leave their pets
20 behind, some vacation rental homes advertise that they are pet friendly. Of course, they **require** security deposits. You never know when Bruno might decide to chew up a sofa!

The pet services industry keeps getting bigger
25 and better, and animals worldwide are loving it. It's no wonder they often look like kings and queens walking down the street. And why not? With all the love and **friendship** pets give us, they **deserve** the very best.

---

4 furry – having a lot of hair/fur
7 booming – growing very quickly
10 grooming – washing, brushing, etc.
13 companion – someone who keeps you company

Questions about the Reading — Choose the best answer.

1. (   ) What is the main idea?
   (A) Animals are good at keeping us company.
   (B) Many people treat their pets like family members.
   (C) Companies make clothes for birds and other pets.
   (D) Dogs and cats do not usually get along.

2. (   ) What is offered by grooming services?
   (A) Food treats
   (B) Designer clothes
   (C) Haircuts
   (D) Pet weddings

3. (   ) What does the article say about pet hotels?
   (A) Their cages are all the same size.
   (B) They are usually very expensive.
   (C) Most of them are only for dogs.
   (D) Some have TVs for pets to watch.

4. (   ) What is suggested about people who rent out vacation homes?
   (A) Though they don't mind animals, they have to protect their property.
   (B) Many also rent out cages for visitors' pets.
   (C) Few have problems with damage caused by dogs or other animals.
   (D) It's uncommon for their houses to have sofas.

5. (   ) What does the word *masters* in line 6 mean?
   (A) teachers
   (B) experts
   (C) owners
   (D) majors

Writing about the Article — Answer each question based on the article.

1. What kinds of clothes can people buy for their pets?
   People can _____.

2. What do pet hotels do?
   They watch pets while _____.

3. Why do pet friendly vacation homes require a deposit?
   The owners are worried _____.

Vocabulary Building Choose the best word to fill in each blank.

1. You work harder than anyone at the company. You _____ to be promoted to manager.
   (A) deserve   (B) continue   (C) spend   (D) fill

2. This is a _____ restaurant. Isn't it expensive?
   (A) common   (B) friendly   (C) fancy   (D) little

3. The hotel will _____ us with towels. We don't need to bring any.
   (A) dress   (B) order   (C) provide   (D) include

4. Her _____ is important to me. We get along like sisters.
   (A) friendship   (B) program   (C) service   (D) deposit

5. Eating here is a _____ for us. We can only afford it a few times a year.
   (A) style   (B) fashion   (C) luxury   (D) range

6. Your ring is _____! I've never seen anything so beautiful.
   (A) quick   (B) friendly   (C) common   (D) gorgeous

7. The rental company _____ a driver's license. You can't rent a car without one.
   (A) requires   (B) worries   (C) leaves   (D) watches

8. Believe it or not, my brother wants to raise a(n) _____ pig!
   (A) choice   (B) menu   (C) industry   (D) pet

Phrase Building Write the correct phrase in each blank.

● a bite to eat   ● can't bear to   ● have it all   ● out on the town

Monica _____ leave her dog Foofoo at home. She takes her pet everywhere, including work. Fortunately, Monica is the boss, so that isn't a problem. Whenever she goes out for _____, Foofoo has to go too. That means Monica only eats at pet friendly restaurants. Sometimes, her friends ask her to go _____ with them, but they know what she'll say. If the club or store is pet friendly, then it's fine. Otherwise, Monica would rather stay at home with Foofoo.

Grammar Exercise

Adjectives + Prepositions

Choose the correct word.

Example: We're very grateful (to/for) all your help.
Answer: We're very grateful (to/(for)) all your help.

1. Hiroaki was so happy (to/for) win the award.

2. Jay was tired (at/from) working all day.

3. Are you still nervous (about/for) tomorrow's test?

4. We're interested (from/in) buying the car if the price is good.

5. Our daughter was excited (to/at) meet the singer.

Listening Exercise   Track 8

Listen to the conversation. Then, answer the following questions.

1. (   ) What are the people going to do?
   (A) Sell a pet
   (B) Meet a neighbor
   (C) Take a trip
   (D) Buy a house

2. (   ) Why doesn't the man want to ask a neighbor for help?
   (A) It would be too much trouble.
   (B) Bob already has several animals.
   (C) He doesn't trust his neighbor.
   (D) The two don't get along.

3. (   ) What will the woman do next?
   (A) Visit the pet motel
   (B) Write a review
   (C) Look for information
   (D) Go to her office

Listening Activity Track 9

Listen to the report. Then, fill in the information in the chart.

1. What kind of animal is Alex?	
2. What do Alex and Martin ride?	
3. What does Alex do during each trip?	
4. Who waves to Alex and his owner?	
5. What might Alex and Martin make?	

Discussion Questions

1. In your opinion, should people be allowed to take pets into any public building? How about movie theaters? Hospitals?

2. Most people raise dogs and cats. Some raise mice and other small animals. What's the strangest animal you've heard of someone raising?

3. Almost every city has some stray dogs and cats. What should be done about them?

Discussion Activity

Design a pet hotel. What animals will you keep? How big will the cages be? Will you offer any special services (like haircuts)? Finally, what will you call your hotel?

Example: Our pet hotel is called The Happy Cat. We will only keep cats. So, there will be lots of toys in every cage....

Pre-Reading Questions
Discuss these questions in pairs.

1. What countries are famous for their fashion?

2. Who are some famous designers? (Ex: Versace)

3. When buying clothes, do you care about the brand? Why or why not?

Consider the Topic
Read each statement. Check if you agree or disagree with it.

	agree	disagree
1. I spend a lot of money on clothes.	☐	☐
2. I like to read fashion magazines.	☐	☐
3. Designer clothes are worth the high cost.	☐	☐

Reading Passage Track 10

1 Armani. Gucci. Valentino. These names are legends of high **fashion**. They're among the top Italian design houses which lead the fashion world. From jackets to bags to accessories, Italy's fashion kings **deliver** the best in fine culture and style.

5 Many Italian design houses, such as Fendi, started as **tiny** family-run businesses. Because of the quality of their work, their **reputations** quickly grew. In 1951, things really **took off** for the Italian fashion industry. That year, a show including 10 **firms** was held in Florence, Italy. It received worldwide attention, and the industry never looked back.

10 Every year, designers show off their newest works in Milan and Paris. These shows are covered in thousands of newspapers, magazines, and TV programs. Movie stars also attend award shows and **weddings** wearing clothes from the great fashion houses. Sometimes, they even wear new **outfits** in the movies. The tuxedo in the Jackie Chan film *The Tuxedo* was an Armani design.

15 In many parts of the world, the importance of Italian fashion is growing. Shows have been held from North America to Asia. And, in November 2007, Valentino took part in a show in Abu Dhabi. He was helping **promote** Italian fashion in the Middle East.

Well **aware of** their brand power, the top design
20 firms have **branched into** other areas. That includes eye glasses, watches, and even hotels. It all adds up to huge profits, with about 48 billion euros in yearly sales. The Gucci Group is at the front of the pack, with sales of 1.8 billion euros in 2005.

25 In addition to many small shops, the great fashion houses have opened large showrooms in Japan, the USA, and elsewhere. For people who want to look their best, these palaces of Italy's modern kings are not just shops. They're celebrations of quality, taste,
30 and style.

[1] legend – something that's very famous
[3] accessories – things worn with an outfit (Ex: gloves)
[14] tuxedo – men's formal suit

[22] euro – currency of the European Union
[28] palace – large house (often for a king)
[29] celebration – happy event to honor or enjoy something

Questions about the Reading

Choose the best answer.

1. (   ) How were family-run companies (like Fendi) able to grow?
      (A) They had great marketing.
      (B) They sold cheap products.
      (C) They made things very well.
      (D) They had beautiful stores.

2. (   ) Which of the following is NOT true about the 1951 show?
      (A) It was held in Florence, Italy.
      (B) Only members of the Italian press knew about it.
      (C) Ten design companies took part.
      (D) It was important in the history of Italian fashion.

3. (   ) Who designed a tuxedo for a movie?
      (A) Jackie Chan
      (B) Valentino
      (C) Gucci
      (D) Armani

4. (   ) What does the word *houses* in line 2 mean?
      (A) companies
      (B) malls
      (C) stocks
      (D) addresses

5. (   ) What does the article suggest about large Italian design firms?
      (A) Many are branching into the restaurant business.
      (B) Most are happy to focus on selling clothes.
      (C) All of their large showrooms are in Italy.
      (D) Some are looking for new ways to make money.

Writing about the Article

Answer each question based on the article.

1. Where are important fashion shows held every year?

   They are held _____ .

2. What did Valentino do in the Middle East?

   In Abu Dhabi, he _____ .

3. How much is the Italian fashion industry worth?

   It is worth _____ .

Vocabulary Building   Choose the best word to fill in each blank.

1. I've never seen you wear that _____. Is it new?
   (A) outfit   (B) program   (C) culture   (D) attention

2. We're a small _____, with only seven employees.
   (A) firm   (B) profit   (C) style   (D) jacket

3. The store is _____. No more than five customers can fit inside.
   (A) modern   (B) quick   (C) tiny   (D) front

4. The man who makes my shirts has a great _____. A friend recommended him to me.
   (A) industry   (B) attention   (C) quality   (D) reputation

5. Please _____ the package before 11:00 so I can be here to receive it.
   (A) include   (B) cover   (C) deliver   (D) attend

6. It was a beautiful _____. I was so happy to see them finally get married.
   (A) award   (B) wedding   (C) design   (D) industry

7. Vera has a great _____ sense. Her clothes and shoes always match.
   (A) showroom   (B) magazine   (C) world   (D) fashion

8. The singer visited the store to _____ his new CD. Many people went to see him.
   (A) attend   (B) promote   (C) grow   (D) start

Phrase Building   Write the correct phrase in each blank. (Remember to use the correct word form.)

● show off   ● aware of   ● branch into   ● take off

Pablo Ciani was a smart businessman. He was _____ the need for a company to change and grow. Pablo owned a clothing store which sold suits and formal wear. He wanted to _____ casual wear, to attract younger people. Rico, his son, suggested that his father open a second store and sell designer clothing. His father agreed. Within three months, the new store's business _____. It was so successful that Pablo opened a third store in less than a year.

Grammar Exercise

Elsewhere, Everywhere, and Nowhere

Fill in each blank with *elsewhere*, *everywhere*, **or** *nowhere*.

Example: We have employees from Spain, India, and _____.
Answer: We have employees from Spain, India, and *elsewhere*.

1. The showroom is _____ near my house. It's an hour's drive away.

2. There are bookstores _____ around here. Finding one will be easy.

3. This shop only sells women's clothing. Let's find something for Tom _____.

4. There used to be just a few Gucci showrooms. Now, they're in malls _____.

5. My watch is _____ to be found. I think I lost it.

Listening Exercise   Track 11

Listen to the conversation. Then, answer the following questions.

1. (   ) What does the woman want the man to do?
   (A) Buy her clothes
   (B) Apply for a credit card
   (C) Help improve her style
   (D) Go shopping

2. (   ) What worries the man about designer clothing?
   (A) The style
   (B) The price
   (C) The color
   (D) The fit

3. (   ) What does the woman imply?
   (A) The man has really bad credit.
   (B) The man should trust her.
   (C) The man understands fashion.
   (D) The man must buy many items.

23

Listening Activity 🔘 Track 12

Listen to the report. Then, fill in the information in the chart.

1. Where is the reporter?	
2. What will Fendi probably show?	
3. What is covering some models' jackets?	
4. How much was one of the jackets worth?	
5. What does the reporter want to do?	

Discussion Questions

1. Do you try hard to make your clothes match, so everything goes well together? Or, do you just wear whatever is in the closet?

2. What does it take to be a good fashion designer? Do you need a certain set of skills? Do you need really good ideas? What else?

3. Fashion models are usually tall and thin. What is your opinion about that? Should there be more models of different shapes and sizes?

Discussion Activity

Working with a few classmates, design an item of clothing. It can be anything – a dress, coat, jacket, or even a pair of shoes. Draw your design on a blank piece of paper and introduce it to the class. You don't need to add color, but if you have pens or markers, then feel free to have fun!

Example: We designed a winter coat. It's white with five buttons. There are two pockets on the outside and one on the inside....

Discuss these questions in pairs.

1. Do you like to read any Internet forums, blogs, or websites?

2. Do you have your own blog or website?

3. Have you seen any funny photos or videos recently?

Consider the Topic

Read each statement. Check if you agree or disagree with it.

	agree	disagree
1. I use a free e-mail account (like Yahoo or Gmail).	☐	☐
2. I pay more attention to ads if they are funny.	☐	☐
3. I often recommend good products and services to friends.	☐	☐

Reading Passage Track 13

1 Companies are always **on the lookout** for new ways to sell products. We're used to seeing ads in newspapers and on television. In recent years, a new type of ad **strategy** – viral marketing – has become popular. It uses the power of the Internet to **spread** information about a product or service.

5 Viral marketing has a "word of mouth" **effect**. The idea is to get people to recommend a product to others. On the Internet, that can be done via e-mail messages. Or, the information may be posted on forums, blogs, and other websites.

Advertisers can't **force** people to spread their 10 message. So, they must think of creative ways to get people to help out. One good strategy is to give something away. For example, when somebody sends an e-mail using a Hotmail account, there's an ad on the bottom. It tells others 15 how to get a free account. Since Hotmail **launched** in 1996, millions of people have signed up for the service. Other companies give away branded screensavers, wallpaper, and sounds. Whenever they're seen or **shared**, it advertises the product.

20 Funny and interesting videos work well as viral marketing tools. When someone **comes across** a great ad for BMW, they may send a link to their friends. They may even add the video to a forum or blog. Companies love the effect. It gets more people to watch their ads, visit their websites, and, hopefully, buy their products.

25 **Unfortunately**, it's hard to plan a viral marketing campaign. There are many ads and websites on the Internet. So, designers and marketers must **think up** creative new strategies. If something is funny, interesting, or **useful** enough, people from Seattle to Seoul will tell their friends about it. If it includes giving something away, the campaign may be even more successful.

¹⁷ branded – carrying a product's logo or company name
¹⁸ screensaver – image that appears when a computer isn't used for a period of time
²⁵ campaign – operation or planned series of activities

Questions about the Reading   Choose the best answer.

1. (   ) What is the main idea?
   (A) The best viral marketers have backgrounds in sales.
   (B) Companies spend too little money on viral marketing.
   (C) If done well, online viral marketing can be successful.
   (D) Newspaper and magazine ads all use viral marketing.

2. (   ) Why do companies give away screensavers and wallpaper?
   (A) To thank people for doing so much to help them
   (B) To advertise a product
   (C) To get people to sign up for an e-mail account
   (D) To learn about customers

3. (   ) What does the article suggest about viral marketing?
   (A) It only works with young customers.
   (B) It was first used by Hotmail.
   (C) It is a fairly new type of marketing.
   (D) It helps many car companies.

4. (   ) What is NOT a tool used by viral marketers?
   (A) Giving things away
   (B) Posting interesting ads
   (C) Calling people up
   (D) Making funny videos

5. (   ) Why is it hard for a viral marketing campaign to succeed?
   (A) People see many ads on the Net every day.
   (B) The cost is very high.
   (C) Advertisers don't understand the Internet.
   (D) Few people shop online.

Writing about the Article   Answer each question based on the article.

1. How do people spread information on the Internet?

   They post _____ .

2. What does the ad on the bottom of a Hotmail message do?

   It tells people _____ .

3. What kinds of videos work well in viral marketing campaigns?

   Videos that are _____ .

27

Vocabulary Building
Choose the best word to fill in each blank.

1. The company _____ 12 years ago, starting with three employees.
   (A) launched (B) forced (C) advertised (D) shared

2. The memo from the boss had a big _____ on everyone. In the future, we will work harder!
   (A) service (B) message (C) account (D) effect

3. Part of our marketing _____ will be building a better website.
   (A) product (B) strategy (C) tool (D) ad

4. If you're hungry, I'll _____ my sandwich with you.
   (A) include (B) spread (C) tell (D) share

5. We can't _____ people to buy the product. However, we can explain to them why they need it.
   (A) post (B) force (C) think (D) look

6. I wish I could help you. _____, I don't have the time.
   (A) Whenever (B) Hopefully (C) So (D) Unfortunately

7. It's a very _____ watch. It tells time and can hold 1,000 phone numbers.
   (A) funny (B) difficult (C) branded (D) useful

8. The problem is _____ quickly. We need to stop it now.
   (A) spreading (B) becoming (C) sending (D) watching

Phrase Building
Write the correct phrase in each blank. (Remember to use the correct word form.)

● on the lookout ● give away ● come across ● think up

While looking through the newspaper one day, I _____ an ad for a used car. The car wasn't in great shape, but the price was low. So, I bought it, spent some money on parts, and fixed the car up. Then I had an idea. What if I could buy more cars, work on them, and resell them for a higher price? Currently, I'm _____ for cars that are cheap but fixable. I've even _____ a name for my new company – Carl's Cheap Cars.

Grammar Exercise

Prepositions of Place

Fill in each blank with *at*, *on*, **or** *in*.

Example: I read about the idea _____ the Internet.
Answer: I read about the idea *on* the Internet.

1. Maybe we should put an ad _____ the newspaper.

2. We saw the movie _____ a theater downtown.

3. Which channel did you see it _____?

4. He wrote about his work problems _____ an e-mail.

5. I hear that song _____ the radio at least 10 times a day.

Listening Exercise   Track 14

Listen to the conversation. Then, answer the following questions.

1. (   ) How did the woman find out about the ad?
   (A) She received a link in an e-mail.
   (B) She visited the company's website.
   (C) She went onto an Internet forum.
   (D) She heard about it at a supermarket.

2. (   ) What does the woman imply about the ad?
   (A) It is serious.
   (B) It is funny.
   (C) It is long.
   (D) It is old.

3. (   ) What is the man thinking about doing?
   (A) Buying something for a friend
   (B) Showing the ad to someone else
   (C) Getting some coffee for the woman
   (D) Waking up late the next day

Listening Activity 🔘 Track 15

Listen to the report. Then, fill in the information in the chart.

1. What product does the company sell?	
2. What did the campaign start with?	
3. What did people need to go onto the special website?	
4. What was on the website?	
5. What was first prize?	

Discussion Questions

1. How often do your friends send you funny photos or links to videos? Can you think of any that you recently received?

2. What free services can you get on the Internet? Do they always carry some kind of ad?

3. Advertising is everywhere: on the Internet, on TV, in magazines, and so on. How do you feel about seeing so many ads every day?

Discussion Activity

You and several classmates work for a movie company. Your new film, *Office Romance*, is about to come out. Now you want everyone on the Internet to know about it. Plan a viral marketing campaign. Think of ways to get people to spread news about the movie. After you're done, share your ideas with the rest of the class.

Example: We'll start by putting three movie previews on YouTube. Then, we'll go onto some forums to post links to the videos....

Pre-Reading Questions
Discuss these questions in pairs.

1. What are your favorite sports?

2. How often do you watch sports on TV?

3. Do any overseas sports teams have players from your country?

Consider the Topic
Read each statement. Check if you agree or disagree with it.

	agree	disagree
1. In my country, many NBA games are shown on TV.	☐	☐
2. I'm a fan of teams with players from my country.	☐	☐
3. Having players from many countries makes a sports league better.	☐	☐

Reading Passage ◎ Track 16

1   The NBA is the USA's top basketball league. Since
     1946, its high-flying **superstars** have amazed fans
     with their speed, skill, and shooting. In recent years,
     the NBA has worked hard to make itself more
5   international. Teams have traveled the world looking
     for talented players. And, the league has held events
     from Europe to Asia to promote the sport.

     During the 2006-2007 season, there were 83
     international players in the NBA, making up about
10   20% of all players. They included some of the league's
     top stars. Dirk Nowitzki, from Germany, even won
     the Most **Valuable** Player (MVP) award in 2007.
     But he was **far from** the first MVP born outside the USA. From 2001-2007,
     international players won the award five out of six years.

15   These **global** superstars have helped make the game more **popular**. In 2002,
     Yao Ming – China's top player – started playing for the Houston Rockets.
     That helped raise interest in the sport in China. There are now 52 TV networks
     showing NBA games there, leading to big **revenues** for the league.

     International players also help their teams sell more shirts, hats, and other
20   products. Such **items** are sold in more than 100,000 stores worldwide. **On top
     of** that, the NBA has advertising **deals** with restaurants, car companies, and
     many other global firms.

     To showcase their talent, NBA teams often travel abroad to play in **exhibition**
     games. During the 2007-2008 preseason, games were held in eight overseas
25   cities, including London, Rome, and Shanghai. Besides playing against each
     other, NBA teams **took on** local teams.

     As the NBA becomes more international, the quality of play keeps rising.
     Styles and strategies that are popular overseas are affecting game play in the
     USA. That makes every player better, no matter where he's from. For sure, it's
30   a golden age for the sport, and an exciting time to be a fan.

---

² amaze – greatly impress   ²⁴ preseason – warm-up before the regular season
²³ showcase – display   ²⁸ strategies – plans and methods

Questions about the Reading   Choose the best answer.

1. (   ) What is the main idea?
   - (A) One of the NBA's best players is from Germany.
   - (B) Every year, there are NBA exhibition games held outside the USA.
   - (C) The quality of play in the NBA is getting better and better.
   - (D) As it becomes more international, the NBA's popularity is growing.

2. (   ) What did Dirk Nowitzki do in 2007?
   - (A) He became the NBA's first international player.
   - (B) He moved to Germany.
   - (C) He traveled to Europe for a preseason game.
   - (D) He won a major award.

3. (   ) How many television networks in China show NBA games?
   - (A) 20
   - (B) 52
   - (C) 83
   - (D) 100,000

4. (   ) What is true about the style of play in the NBA?
   - (A) It is being influenced by international players.
   - (B) It is becoming less exciting than it once was.
   - (C) It is affecting the strategies of overseas teams.
   - (D) It is improving for just a few of the stars.

5. (   ) What is NOT a way international players help teams?
   - (A) Through tourism dollars
   - (B) Through television revenues
   - (C) Through advertising deals
   - (D) Through product sales

Writing about the Article   Answer each question based on the article.

1. When did Yao Ming start playing in the NBA?

   He started _____.

2. What kinds of companies does the NBA have advertising deals with?

   It has deals with _____.

3. What were some cities that hosted 2007-2008 preseason games?

   There were games in _____.

Listening Activity Track 18

Listen to the report. Then, fill in the information in the chart.

1. When did the game take place?	
2. Where was it held?	
3. Where is Manu Ginobili from?	
4. How many members of his fan club attended?	
5. How long did Ginobili stay after the game?	

Discussion Questions

1. Some people like playing sports. Others prefer to watch. And, some like to do both. How about you?

2. Most NBA players are very tall. To be a good basketball player, does a person need to be big and strong? Why or why not?

3. Many young people admire sports stars. Do professional athletes make good role models for children? Why or why not?

Discussion Activity

Make a small list of sports and games from your country. Choose one and think of ways to make it more popular overseas. First, how will you teach people in other countries about the sport or game? Next, how will you help it become popular overseas?

Example: Australian rules football is a popular sport here, but few people in other countries know about it. First, we will build a website that teaches people about the sport....

Grammar Exercise

Verb Form

Write the correct form of the verb in parentheses.

Example: My boss is (look) _____ for a new assistant.
Answer: My boss is *looking* for a new assistant.

1. I have (call) _____ every phone number here. None of them is Mr. Taro's.

2. If you want to (attract) _____ young people, you should play more pop music.

3. Did you try (ask) _____ Elizabeth for help?

4. I'm excited about (travel) _____ to Indonesia next month.

5. The ring was (give) _____ to me by my mother.

Listening Exercise   Track 17

Listen to the conversation. Then, answer the following questions.

1. (   ) Where will the game be held?
    (A) New York
    (B) Singapore
    (C) California
    (D) Hong Kong

2. (   ) What does the woman think will happen?
    (A) The tickets will cost a lot.
    (B) The game won't sell out.
    (C) The players won't try hard.
    (D) The event will be boring.

3. (   ) What is the man thinking about doing?
    (A) Watching the event on TV
    (B) Inviting his friend to play basketball
    (C) Taking a trip to the USA
    (D) Attending the game in person

Listening Activity 🔵 Track 18

Listen to the report. Then, fill in the information in the chart.

1. When did the game take place?	
2. Where was it held?	
3. Where is Manu Ginobili from?	
4. How many members of his fan club attended?	
5. How long did Ginobili stay after the game?	

Discussion Questions

1. Some people like playing sports. Others prefer to watch. And, some like to do both. How about you?

2. Most NBA players are very tall. To be a good basketball player, does a person need to be big and strong? Why or why not?

3. Many young people admire sports stars. Do professional athletes make good role models for children? Why or why not?

Discussion Activity

Make a small list of sports and games from your country. Choose one and think of ways to make it more popular overseas. First, how will you teach people in other countries about the sport or game? Next, how will you help it become popular overseas?

Example: Australian rules football is a popular sport here, but few people in other countries know about it. First, we will build a website that teaches people about the sport....

Questions about the Reading   Choose the best answer.

1. (   ) What is the main idea?
   (A) One of the NBA's best players is from Germany.
   (B) Every year, there are NBA exhibition games held outside the USA.
   (C) The quality of play in the NBA is getting better and better.
   (D) As it becomes more international, the NBA's popularity is growing.

2. (   ) What did Dirk Nowitzki do in 2007?
   (A) He became the NBA's first international player.
   (B) He moved to Germany.
   (C) He traveled to Europe for a preseason game.
   (D) He won a major award.

3. (   ) How many television networks in China show NBA games?
   (A) 20
   (B) 52
   (C) 83
   (D) 100,000

4. (   ) What is true about the style of play in the NBA?
   (A) It is being influenced by international players.
   (B) It is becoming less exciting than it once was.
   (C) It is affecting the strategies of overseas teams.
   (D) It is improving for just a few of the stars.

5. (   ) What is NOT a way international players help teams?
   (A) Through tourism dollars
   (B) Through television revenues
   (C) Through advertising deals
   (D) Through product sales

Writing about the Article   Answer each question based on the article.

1. When did Yao Ming start playing in the NBA?

   He started _____ .

2. What kinds of companies does the NBA have advertising deals with?

   It has deals with _____ .

3. What were some cities that hosted 2007-2008 preseason games?

   There were games in _____ .

Vocabulary Building

Choose the best word to fill in each blank.

1. Basketball is a _____ sport. A lot of kids play at the park after school.
   (A) high   (B) talented   (C) valuable   (D) popular

2. This month, the museum is holding a(n) _____ of Brazilian art.
   (A) skill   (B) exhibition   (C) firm   (D) sport

3. Starbucks is a(n) _____ company. It has coffee shops in many countries.
   (A) global   (B) recent   (C) affected   (D) outer

4. _____ athletes often earn millions of dollars per year.
   (A) Superstar   (B) Award   (C) Preseason   (D) Event

5. Our total _____ were up 15% this year. We should get a bonus.
   (A) leagues   (B) seasons   (C) worlds   (D) revenues

6. We made a(n) _____ with a sports magazine. We'll help them sell copies of the magazine, and they'll give us free ad space.
   (A) award   (B) deal   (C) interest   (D) style

7. Charlie is a(n) _____ employee. I hope he doesn't retire this year.
   (A) valuable   (B) recent   (C) hard   (D) international

8. You left one _____ off the list – the tall glass cabinet.
   (A) strategy   (B) event   (C) quality   (D) item

Phrase Building

Write the correct phrase in each blank. (Remember to use the correct word form.)

● make up   ● on top of   ● take on   ● far from

When we first started our furniture business, times were hard. With six employees and very little money, we _____ some very large and wealthy companies. It was _____ easy, but we worked hard. With good service and great quality, we won many customers. These days, our business is successful. However, _____ material costs (especially wood), our shipping and rental costs are high. So, we still need to be careful with money.

Pre-Reading Questions   Discuss these questions in pairs.

1. How can you learn about the latest celebrity news?

2. When the press gossips about celebrities, what kinds of things do they report on?

3. Which famous people does the press like to gossip about?

Consider the Topic   Read each statement. Check if you agree or disagree with it.

	agree	disagree
1. I am interested in the lives of my favorite stars.	☐	☐
2. The press has the right to photograph stars, no matter where they are.	☐	☐
3. Most gossip about celebrities is true.	☐	☐

Reading Passage 🔘 Track 19

1   Are you **curious** about the private lives of actors and pop stars? If so, you're
not alone. Every day, the world's newspapers, magazines, and websites
deliver a **constant** stream of **gossip** about the rich and famous. Although it's
sometimes called "junk food news," celebrity gossip is more popular than
5   ever.

   Movie stars, athletes, singers, and politicians are the favorite subjects of the
gossip **media**. Because they're always **in the public eye**, people feel very
close to these superstars. We want to know what they're doing, what clothes
they're wearing, and who they're spending time with. In offices, chatrooms,
10 and coffee shops, celebrity news is a common topic of conversation.

   There's even a class of photographer, the "paparazzi," that follows celebrities
around. Wherever stars eat, shop, or travel, the paparazzi are always there,
cameras in hand. Some people see this as an invasion of privacy. However,
stars can benefit from the paparazzi, whose photos are sold to news sources.
15 It keeps stars in the public eye, which helps their **careers**.

   Stories in the gossip media may be based on public facts, information from
stars' friends, or secret "insider" sources. **Regardless of** how crazy the

stories are, stars usually **ignore** them. However, they
sometimes fight back. In Hollywood and London,
20 there are special lawyers who work for celebrities.
They may sue a magazine for printing a false story or
demand that photographs not be printed.

   In today's world, the media is everywhere. It's
impossible for stars to hide from the press. At
25 the same time, it's hard for the rest of us to avoid
celebrity news. Yet, **at the end of the day**, we have
only ourselves to **blame**. As a famous magazine
editor once said, celebrity gossip is everywhere
because we have such a huge appetite for it.

---

4 celebrity – famous person
6 athlete – person who plays a sport
6 politician – elected government worker
13 invasion – attack

17 insider – person who works in an industry
28 editor – supervisor for a newspaper,
      magazine, etc.
29 appetite – hunger

Questions about the Reading — Choose the best answer.

1. (   ) What is the main idea?
(A) Celebrity gossip is popular because of the high demand for it.
(B) Movie stars have more interesting lives than the rest of us.
(C) The media doesn't focus enough on important news stories.
(D) The gossip media is spreading faster on the Internet than on TV.

2. (   ) What do the paparazzi do?
(A) They cause trouble for photographers.
(B) They protect the privacy of stars.
(C) They buy images from news sources.
(D) They take photos of celebrities.

3. (   ) Which type of celebrity is NOT mentioned in the article?
(A) Professional athletes
(B) Novel writers
(C) Famous politicians
(D) Pop stars

4. (   ) What do special lawyers do for famous stars?
(A) Print stories that are 100% true
(B) Create gossip about the media
(C) Help protect them from the press
(D) Tell them which gossip to spread

5. (   ) What does the article suggest about the media?
(A) It is a common part of our daily lives.
(B) It helps us hide from celebrity news.
(C) It is less powerful than it once was.
(D) It doesn't give the public what it wants.

Writing about the Article — Answer each question based on the article.

1. Where do people talk about celebrities?
   They talk about them in _____ .

2. How do stars benefit from the paparazzi?
   The paparazzi help _____ .

3. What are some cities with special celebrity lawyers?
   They can be found _____ .

Vocabulary Building   Choose the best word to fill in each blank.

1. A _____ as an airplane pilot would be really interesting.
   (A) conversation   (B) career   (C) source   (D) press

2. Finishing the job by that date is _____. There isn't enough time.
   (A) impossible   (B) alone   (C) public   (D) major

3. As the Internet grows, other types of _____ are becoming less popular.
   (A) media   (B) privacy   (C) appetite   (D) celebrity

4. Let's not look for someone to _____. Let's just solve the problem.
   (A) follow   (B) demand   (C) spend   (D) blame

5. Thank you for the present. I'm so _____ to see what it is!
   (A) famous   (B) huge   (C) special   (D) curious

6. I tried to _____ the noise, but it was too loud.
   (A) wear   (B) benefit   (C) ignore   (D) feel

7. Since we live in a big city, traffic is a(n) _____ problem.
   (A) constant   (B) false   (C) same   (D) alone

8. Spreading too much _____ about your colleagues may get you into
   trouble.
   (A) class   (B) media   (C) gossip   (D) world

Phrase Building   Write the correct phrase in each blank.

● fight back   ● at the end of the day   ● in the public eye   ● regardless of

After Florence married a famous baseball player,
she was always _____. The press
followed her around. They wanted to know
everything about her life. _____
how politely she asked, they would not leave her
alone. For a few months, it bothered her. Later,
she decided that, _____, there
was nothing she could do about the situation. So,
Florence stopped trying to avoid the press. She
let them take photos and interview her. She even
became friends with some reporters.

Grammar Exercise

However, Wherever, and Whatever

Fill in each blank with *however*, *wherever*, **or** *whatever*.

Example: I want to buy it. _____, I left my wallet at home.
Answer: I want to buy it. *However*, I left my wallet at home.

1. It's your birthday. We can go _____ you want.

2. Ask me _____ you like. I'll answer any question.

3. The dog follows her _____ she goes. It's kind of strange!

4. It's late, true. _____, I still want to go bowling.

5. _____ the price is, I'll pay it. I simply must have it!

Listening Exercise   Track 20

Listen to the conversation. Then, answer the following questions.

1. (   ) What does the article say about Brad Pitt?
   (A) He went on a long vacation.
   (B) He made a movie overseas.
   (C) He took an expensive trip.
   (D) He earned $30,000 in one day.

2. (   ) What does the man think Brad Pitt should do?
   (A) End his acting career
   (B) Be nicer to his fans
   (C) Try to spend less money
   (D) Leave the media alone

3. (   ) How does the woman react to the man's idea?
   (A) She doesn't believe it's possible.
   (B) She thinks Pitt should give it a try.
   (C) She says she has had the same idea.
   (D) She wants the man to explain it.

41

Listening Activity 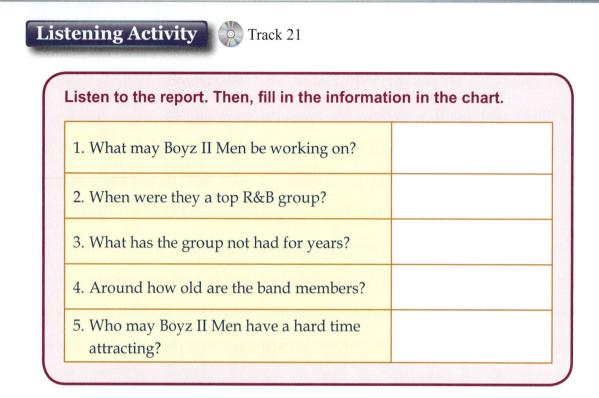 Track 21

Listen to the report. Then, fill in the information in the chart.

1. What may Boyz II Men be working on?	
2. When were they a top R&B group?	
3. What has the group not had for years?	
4. Around how old are the band members?	
5. Who may Boyz II Men have a hard time attracting?	

Discussion Questions

1. In your opinion, why are people so interested in the private lives of celebrities?

2. Does the media treat the stars fairly? In other words, do they try to bring us every side of a story, or just the exciting parts?

3. Are there limits to what the press should gossip about? Should some subjects and types of information be kept out of the news?

Discussion Activity

Make up a gossip story about a celebrity. Decide if it will be a singer, movie star, or other famous person. What will the story be about? Where will you get your information? Do you have any photos? Once you're finished, share your gossip with the class!

Example: We've got some interesting news about Will Smith. The superstar was seen in England last week. You won't believe what he was doing there....

Pre-Reading Questions

Discuss these questions in pairs.

1. Would you rather work at a company or start your own business?

2. What would someone need to start a SOHO?

3. What kinds of work are suitable for a SOHO?

Consider the Topic

Read each statement. Check if you agree or disagree with it.

	agree	disagree
1. I prefer to make my own work schedule.	☐	☐
2. I don't need a manager. I can work hard without a boss watching over me.	☐	☐
3. I don't mind working on nights and weekends.	☐	☐

Reading Passage Track 22

1   Many people in Taiwan want to be their own boss. Setting up a SOHO is a low-cost way to make that **happen**. A wide variety of jobs, from design work to sales, can be done as a one-man or one-woman operation. With a small amount of space and a lot of hard work, a SOHO can be a great way
5   to **earn a living**.

The first step is to decide what type of work you'll do. That will depend on your skill set. Are you good with computers? Then you could build websites. Are you **artistic**? Then design work or drawing may be the right choice. If you have a good idea but don't have the skills, taking a class or
10   two might **do the trick**.

Next, make sure you have the right **equipment**. That will **vary** for each SOHO, but you'll probably need a computer with an Internet connection. A fax machine is also a good idea. If possible, set up your office in its own room, not in your bedroom or living room. According to experts, that
15   creates a better working environment.

Now you're ready to look for **clients**. An ad in the newspaper or online is a good start. Telling friends that you've set up a company can also help you **network**. When the big day comes and you start meeting clients, make sure to dress well. A professional **image** goes a long way towards
20   winning a client's trust and business.

When running a SOHO, remember that the most important person is YOU. That means a lot of hard work, often on nights and weekends. If you do a good job (and meet your **deadlines**), then clients will come
25   back again and again. They'll also recommend you to friends. Once **word of mouth** about your excellent company spreads, you won't need to look for clients. They'll start looking for you.

¹ SOHO - Small Office, Home Office

Questions about the Reading   Choose the best answer.

1. (   ) What does the article suggest about running a SOHO?
   (A) Only a few kinds of work are suitable for a SOHO.
   (B) Clients will always come back with more job offers.
   (C) The type of SOHO one starts depends on one's skills.
   (D) Fax machines are more important than computers.

2. (   ) Which of the following jobs is NOT mentioned in the article?
   (A) Reporter
   (B) Artist
   (C) Salesperson
   (D) Designer

3. (   ) Why do experts say an office should be in its own room?
   (A) It creates more space in the house.
   (B) It won't bother other family members.
   (C) It is better for getting work done.
   (D) It shows clients a professional image.

4. (   ) What is a good way to find clients?
   (A) Going on a trip with friends
   (B) Putting an ad on the Internet
   (C) Reading books about networking
   (D) Dressing as comfortably as possible

5. (   ) What does the word *operation* in line 3 mean?
   (A) surgery
   (B) attack
   (C) control
   (D) business

Writing about the Article   Answer each question based on the article.

1. What kind of SOHO is recommended for people with computer skills?
   With those skills, _____.

2. What equipment do most SOHOs need?
   SOHOs usually _____.

3. What can a professional image do for you?
   It can help win _____.

45

Vocabulary Building Choose the best word to fill in each blank.

1. Do you want to tell me what _____? I might be able to help.
   (A) depended   (B) happened   (C) remembered   (D) decided

2. Many of our _____ are department stores. We create window displays for them.
   (A) ideas   (B) costs   (C) clients   (D) SOHOs

3. Barry is very _____. He can draw almost anything.
   (A) possible   (B) artistic   (C) wide   (D) ready

4. All the _____ is new. We are able to make CD quality recordings.
   (A) trust   (B) equipment   (C) amount   (D) environment

5. The cost _____ from job to job, depending on how long it will take.
   (A) varies   (B) decides   (C) builds   (D) happens

6. We're trying for a light, friendly _____. So, our name cards are yellow.
   (A) skill   (B) trust   (C) boss   (D) image

7. Next Friday is an impossible _____. It will take me another two weeks.
   (A) client   (B) deadline   (C) business   (D) connection

8. This trade show is a good place to _____. I've made some great contacts here.
   (A) vary   (B) build   (C) recommend   (D) network

Phrase Building Write the correct phrase in each blank.

● do the trick   ● earn a living   ● come back   ● word of mouth

In the retail world, it's hard to _____.
If you have a product that sells well, it's easy for
someone to open a shop next door and sell the same
thing. So, a store needs to make itself different.
Most importantly, it needs to offer a great shopping
experience. Friendly service and a great store design
often _____. Happy customers will
tell their friends about their experience. For a retail
store, good or bad _____ can make or
break a business.

Grammar Exercise

Pronouns

Choose the correct word.

Example: That dog loves to play with (it/its) toys.
Answer: That dog loves to play with (it/its) toys.

1. Are you sure the car is (their/theirs)?

2. I'd like to speak with (him/his) once he's out of the meeting.

3. Did (she/her) say what time Fred was coming back?

4. These sandwiches can't all be for (us/ours). It's too much food for three people!

5. Tell me more about (your/yours) idea.

Listening Exercise Track 23

Listen to the conversation. Then, answer the following questions.

1. (   ) What did the woman hear?
   (A) The T-shirts are all sold out.
   (B) The company has a couple of problems.
   (C) The man's products are popular.
   (D) The online ordering system is excellent.

2. (   ) What does the man say about his company?
   (A) Things are slowly getting better.
   (B) The job is sometimes boring.
   (C) He isn't making much money.
   (D) Work takes up most of his time.

3. (   ) What does the woman imply?
   (A) The man's situation will improve.
   (B) It's a great joy to be married.
   (C) New companies rarely succeed.
   (D) She has never run a business.

Listening Activity Track 24

Listen to the advertisement. Then, fill in the information in the chart.

1. How long does the course take?	
2. How much business experience does the teacher have?	
3. How many classes has he taught?	
4. What will people who take the course get?	
5. What discount can someone get by registering today?	

Discussion Questions

1. What are some positive and negative points about running a SOHO?

2. Sometimes, people with SOHOs have trouble getting money from clients. What's a good way to make sure you get paid?

3. How does the Internet make it easier to run a SOHO?

Discussion Activity

Plan a three-person SOHO. First, decide what type of SOHO you're going to start. Then, decide what tasks each team member will handle. Next, come up with ways to find clients. Finally, think up a company name and draw a company name card.

Example: My friends and I will open a jewelry SOHO. I will design the jewelry. Another partner will take care of the website and handle orders....

Pre-Reading Questions

Discuss these questions in pairs.

1. Why do people cut down forests?

2. In your country, have many forests disappeared in recent years?

3. In what ways are forests important to the environment?

Consider the Topic

Read each statement. Check if you agree or disagree with it.

	agree	disagree
1. Few people are concerned about forests.	☐	☐
2. Whenever a tree is cut down, a new one should be planted.	☐	☐
3. More forests should be cut down to make room for people.	☐	☐

Reading Passage   Track 25

1   The world's **forests** are disappearing. For a number of reasons, that's **cause for alarm**. Governments, NGOs (non-governmental organizations), and private individuals are **taking steps** to **reverse** this trend. Through small and large-scale reforestation activities, they're nursing forests back to life.

5   Every year, some 13 million hectares of forest disappear. In some cases, timber and mining companies are to blame. Other times, forests are cleared to **make room for** new farms. Or, the land may be used to raise livestock.

In some parts of the world, the annual loss is **severe**. From 2000-2005, 4.3 million hectares were lost every year in South America. During the same period, four

10   million hectares were lost annually in Africa. The situation is critical in Vietnam. There, 51 percent of the country's primary forests — meaning forests never touched by human activity — were lost from 2000-2005.

In many places, efforts are underway to restore forests that have been **damaged** or destroyed.

15   The first step is to identify the tree **species** that are native to the area. **Ideally**, a variety of species are planted. That improves an area's biodiversity. Over a period of two years, seedlings are **monitored** to make sure they grow healthily.

20   Reforestation efforts have had mixed results. In the USA, people in Oregon plant between 40 to 50 million trees in their state every year. In Costa Rica, the Cloudbridge River Project is restoring an important section of forest. Some countries, unfortunately, have had less success. Illegal tree harvesting and livestock overgrazing are among the problems they face.

25   Despite such **setbacks**, reforestation efforts are spreading. More countries are becoming aware of the benefits of healthy forests. They improve the soil, stop the spread of deserts, and protect the ground water. Forests also help in the fight against global warming by removing harmful gases from the air. Furthermore, healthy forests make the land more beautiful for future generations.

³ individuals – people
⁴ nursing – bringing back to a healthy state
⁵ timber – wood
¹⁰ critical – very serious

¹⁷ biodiversity – having a variety of
        plants and animals
²⁴ overgrazing – eating too much of an
        area's plants and grass

Questions about the Reading

Choose the best answer.

1. (   ) What is the main idea?
   (A) Mining companies are not concerned about the environment.
   (B) Government efforts to replant trees are rarely effective.
   (C) Though our forests are in trouble, efforts to save them are underway.
   (D) NGOs are the most important groups involved in tree replanting.

2. (   ) What is a reason reforestation is not succeeding in some countries?
   (A) There is too much ground water.
   (B) The new trees are not native to the area.
   (C) People illegally cut down the new trees.
   (D) The soil is not healthy enough.

3. (   ) Why does the article mention the activities in Oregon and Costa Rica?
   (A) To show how such attempts are facing problems
   (B) To give examples of successful reforestation efforts
   (C) To show how forests are good for the environment
   (D) To give examples of unusual NGO activities

4. (   ) What is NOT a reason forests are disappearing?
   (A) Mining companies
   (B) Raising livestock
   (C) Global warming
   (D) Expanding farms

5. (   ) What does the word *harvesting* in line 23 mean?
   (A) gathering
   (B) observing
   (C) planting
   (D) accounting

Writing about the Article

Answer each question based on the article.

1. Why are a variety of tree species planted in an area during reforestation efforts?
   A variety are planted to _____.

2. Why is the disappearance of forests in Vietnam so serious?
   It is serious because _____.

3. How do forests help fight global warming?
   Forests help by _____.

Vocabulary Building   Choose the best word to fill in each blank.

1. After the storm ended, people went outside to look at the _____ it had caused.
   (A) reason   (B) forest   (C) damage   (D) success

2. Many _____ of animals make their homes in the forest.
   (A) activities   (B) states   (C) deserts   (D) species

3. _____, I would like to attend graduate school in Canada.
   (A) Ideally   (B) Severely   (C) Annually   (D) Illegally

4. The school decided to _____ its policy of not allowing hats. We can wear them now.
   (A) disappear   (B) damage   (C) reverse   (D) face

5. Breaking the rules can lead to _____ punishment if you are caught.
   (A) severe   (B) native   (C) lost   (D) global

6. The heavy rains caused a major _____ to the rescue efforts.
   (A) trend   (B) setback   (C) section   (D) benefit

7. While outdoors, parents should _____ young children at all times.
   (A) restore   (B) remove   (C) identify   (D) monitor

8. Almost every summer, we go camping in a redwood _____.
   (A) mining   (B) soil   (C) forest   (D) period

Phrase Building   Write the correct phrase in each blank. (Remember to use the correct word form.)

● make room for   ● cause for alarm   ● take steps   ● mixed results

Between school, family, and friends, many students feel they don't have time to get everything done. However, this isn't a _____. While it's important to do well in school, it's also important to _____ fun activities. As the saying goes, "All work and no play makes Jack a dull boy." By _____ to ensure you have time to both study and relax, you will feel a lot happier.

Grammar Exercise

Other and Another

Fill in each blank with *other* **or** *another*.

Example: We need _____ chair. Can you get one from the living room?

Answer: We need *another* chair. Can you get one from the living room?

1. _____ cities have public skateboard ramps. Why don't we have any?

2. I need _____ five minutes before I'll be ready to go.

3. Are there any _____ students who want to join us?

4. Some of the _____ managers have said they're against the plan.

5. _____ idea would be to plant some fruit trees out back.

Listening Exercise   Track 26

Listen to the conversation. Then, answer the following questions.

1. ( ) How did the woman feel while watching the video?
   (A) She felt angry.
   (B) She felt excited.
   (C) She felt sad.
   (D) She felt tired.

2. ( ) According to the man, why are people replanting trees?
   (A) Trees are important to the environment.
   (B) People need trees to cut down in the future.
   (C) It gives them something to do on weekends.
   (D) The forests are quickly disappearing.

3. ( ) What does the woman want to do?
   (A) Watch another video
   (B) Take a trip to a forest
   (C) Learn about the environment
   (D) Plant some trees

Listening Activity 🔘 Track 27

Listen to the report. Then, fill in the information in the chart.

1. Where are volunteers asked to go?	
2. Who can volunteer?	
3. What kind of business is McGregor's?	
4. What will Mario's Pizza provide for volunteers?	
5. Who should people call for more information?	

Discussion Questions

1. What are some products that come from trees? To help save forests, can they be made using any other materials?

2. Should governments and NGOs handle most reforestation activities? Or, should the companies who cut trees down be required to plant new trees?

3. What can countries which are having problems with reforestation do to improve their success rate?

Discussion Activity

Plan a club at school for students who want to help the environment. First, choose a name for your club. Second, decide which issue you will support. For example, you could make posters with information about an endangered species.

Example: We're going to start a group called the Dolphin Club. Our goal is to get people to pay attention to the shrinking dolphin population. We'll start by building a website....

Pre-Reading Questions

Discuss these questions in pairs.

1. What is your favorite kind of tea?

2. How often do you drink tea?

3. What snacks go well with tea?

Consider the Topic

Read each statement. Check if you agree or disagree with it.

	agree	disagree
1. I drink coffee more often than tea.	☐	☐
2. I like to brew tea using tea leaves and a pot.	☐	☐
3. I like buying tea from tea stalls.	☐	☐

Reading Passage 🔘 Track 28

1   For a long time, tea has been an important part of Taiwan's culture. From oolong tea to bubble tea, there are varieties for every age, taste, and schedule. Taiwan is also the home of the Pinglin Tea Industry Museum, said to be the world's largest. **In the face of** coffee shops opening everywhere, tea
5   still holds a key place in the hearts and lives of Taiwanese people.

Taiwan's climate and geography make it an excellent place to grow tea. The crop has been commercially grown on the island for more than 125 years. For decades, Taiwan was a major tea exporter. However, since the 1970s, the **domestic** market has become more important for local growers. Also, there's
10 a greater **focus** on expensive varieties like Taiwan Tea No. 18. It's a black tea grown in Yuchih Township.

People in Taiwan can enjoy tea at many different places. At traditional tea houses, customers can relax while sipping oolong, paochong, and other varieties.
15 These places also serve snacks like dried fruit and peanuts. Maokong, in the southern hills of Taipei, has many such tea houses, in a beautiful setting. It's hard to **imagine** a more perfect place to take a guest.

For people **on the go**, tea stalls offer dozens of drinks
20 that can be **prepared** in just a few minutes. These shops have helped make black tea very popular in Taiwan. Tea is **mixed** with milk powder and other ingredients to make delicious Taiwanese **inventions** like pearl milk tea.

25 In the 21st century, cities and countries are starting to look more and more **alike**. International stores and restaurants are opening in many places. And, international **brands** are seen on store shelves everywhere. It's nice to have something special, like Taiwan's tea culture, to help a country **stand out** in the crowd.

---

6 climate – common weather for a place   7 commercially – done to make money
6 geography – features of the land   14 sip – drink slowly
7 crop – plant grown for a certain use   19 stalls – small booths/shops

Questions about the Reading   Choose the best answer.

1. (   ) What does Taiwan have that makes it a good place to grow tea?
    (A) Suitable natural features
    (B) Few coffee shops
    (C) Low import taxes
    (D) Many great museums

2. (   ) What is Taiwan Tea No. 18 an example of?
    (A) A drink that is prepared at a stall
    (B) A variety of oolong tea from Taiwan
    (C) A type of tea that costs a lot of money
    (D) A product that is not sold anymore

3. (   ) What has made black tea more popular in Taiwan?
    (A) Tea stalls
    (B) International restaurants
    (C) Coffee shops
    (D) Traditional tea houses

4. (   ) Which of the following is true about tea in Taiwan?
    (A) Black tea has always sold better than oolong tea.
    (B) The Pinglin Tea Industry Museum is in Maokong.
    (C) Tea growers now focus more on the local market.
    (D) Tea was invented in Taiwan about 125 years ago.

5. (   ) What situation are we facing in the 21st century?
    (A) Only a few stores carry international brands.
    (B) Countries now have many things in common.
    (C) Cities are becoming more and more different.
    (D) It's becoming easy to stand out in the crowd.

Writing about the Article   Answer each question based on the article.

1. What is special about the Pinglin Tea Industry Museum?
The museum is _____.

2. Where is Taiwan Tea No. 18 grown?
It is grown _____.

3. What are some snacks sold at traditional tea houses?
They sell _____.

Vocabulary Building   Choose the best word to fill in each blank.

1. After you _____ the tea and milk powder, you add sugar.
   (A) imagine   (B) offer   (C) mix   (D) relax

2. I don't care about a product's _____, just its quality.
   (A) setting   (B) schedule   (C) brand   (D) place

3. You and I are a lot _____. We both love badminton and swimming.
   (A) alike   (B) major   (C) international   (D) traditional

4. Our store sells too many products. We need to put more _____ on a few main lines.
   (A) focus   (B) exporter   (C) variety   (D) decade

5. It's a(n) _____ airline. There are no overseas flights.
   (A) popular   (B) domestic   (C) perfect   (D) expensive

6. Connie didn't _____ well for the test, so she received a low score.
   (A) become   (B) hold   (C) prepare   (D) serve

7. The light bulb was one of the 19th century's most important _____.
   (A) inventions   (B) schedules   (C) exporters   (D) shelves

8. I've never been to Berlin, but I _____ it must be very nice.
   (A) relax   (B) offer   (C) imagine   (D) make

Phrase Building   Write the correct phrase in each blank.

● stand out   ● on the go   ● in the face of   ● part of

Five years ago, there was only one Italian restaurant in the neighborhood. Now there are four. _____ so much competition, each place needs to work hard to _____. One restaurant has added a very interesting feature. It is designed for people _____. Customers can phone in their order or place an order online. Then, they drive up to the restaurant and pick up their meal without leaving their car. So far, the service has been very popular.

Grammar Exercise

Since, For, and Until

Fill in each blank with *since, for,* **or** *until.*

Example: We have been friends _____ 10 years.
Answer: We have been friends *for* 10 years.

1. I will wait here _____ it stops raining.

2. We have lived in Kaohsiung _____ 1983.

3. They have worked at the same company _____ most of their lives.

4. The guard stands there every day _____ 10:00 PM.

5. That car dealership has been open _____ the 1950s.

Listening Exercise Track 29

Listen to the conversation. Then, answer the following questions.

1. (   ) How long has the man been in Taiwan?
   (A) One day
   (B) A few days
   (C) A few weeks
   (D) One month

2. (   ) What does the man usually drink?
   (A) Pearl milk tea
   (B) Coffee
   (C) Black tea
   (D) Hot water

3. (   ) What does the woman say about pearl milk tea?
   (A) It's very cheap.
   (B) It's not well known.
   (C) It's a kind of dessert.
   (D) It's fun to drink.

Listening Activity   🔘 Track 30

Listen to the report. Then, fill in the information in the chart.

1. What kind of drinks is the report about?	
2. What can drinking too much milk tea lead to?	
3. What should you do if you drink a lot of milk tea?	
4. How much sugar should people ask for?	
5. What problem may be caused by drinking tea late at night?	

Discussion Questions

1. Which do you prefer – buying drinks at convenience stores, drink stalls, or tea houses?

2. Some people like cold drinks, and others only drink hot beverages. How about you?

3. Drinking tea is one of Taiwan's many interesting traditions. What special traditions and customs does your country have?

Discussion Activity

Plan a day trip for a foreign guest to your city or town. Where will you go? What kinds of food will you introduce him or her to? And, of course, what tea drinks will you recommend?

Example: In the morning, we will eat at a famous breakfast shop in the center of the city. Their milk tea is excellent....

Pre-Reading Questions
Discuss these questions in pairs.

1. How do people become very rich?

2. What would you do with your money if you were super rich?

3. Have you ever given money to a charity or done volunteer work?

Consider the Topic
Read each statement. Check if you agree or disagree with it.

	agree	disagree
1. Most people want to earn a lot of money.	☐	☐
2. It's important to help other people when we can.	☐	☐
3. Rich people should give some of their money to charity.	☐	☐

1   Most billionaires work hard to build their fortunes. With the money they earn, they can buy large homes, expensive cars, and private airplanes. But even after spending millions of dollars, they still have huge amounts of money. What do they do with it?

5   **Charity** has always been an **option**. About 100 years ago, Andrew Carnegie, the world's richest man at the time, gave away most of his money. His gifts went to thousands of libraries, schools, and other groups. Another big giver of the past century was John D. Rockefeller. He **donated** money to hospitals, universities, and other charities.

10   In recent years, we've seen a new group of super givers. At the top of the list is Bill Gates. In 1994, using money from his Microsoft fortune, he set up the William & Melinda Gates Foundation. The foundation first helped US libraries get connected to the Internet.

15   Then, it turned to fighting **diseases** like AIDS and malaria in poor countries. From 1994 to 2007, the foundation gave away more than $13 billion.

In 2006, Warren Buffet **announced** that he too was **giving away** most of his money. With a fortune of

20   more than $40 billion, Buffet **admired** what Bill and Melinda Gates were doing. So, under Buffet's plan, 5/6 of the money that he is donating will go to the Gates Foundation.

Will more of the super rich become philanthropists? There is some doubt. Every year, *Forbes* magazine puts out a list of the world's richest people.

25   Some people believe that billionaires care about their place on the list. To keep a high spot, they may **hold onto** their money. However, with the recent donations of Gates and others, that **trend** may start to **turn around**. More **wealthy** people may try for a high spot on the list of super givers.

---

¹ billionaire – person with one billion dollars
¹ fortune – large amount of money
¹³ foundation – group that manages donations
¹⁶ malaria – a disease spread by mosquitoes
²³ philanthropist – person who gives away a lot of money

Questions about the Reading
Choose the best answer.

1. (   ) What is the article mainly about?
    (A) The generous actions of very rich philanthropists
    (B) The differences between past and present givers
    (C) The best ways to donate large amounts of money
    (D) The influence of the *Forbes* list on charity donations

2. (   ) What is suggested about Andrew Carnegie?
    (A) He wanted most of his fortune to go to schools.
    (B) He donated money to a lot of different causes.
    (C) He is one of the biggest givers of the 21st century.
    (D) He did not encourage others to give to charity.

3. (   ) How much did the Gates Foundation give away in its first 13 years?
    (A) $1 billion
    (B) $13 billion
    (C) $40 billion
    (D) $48 billion

4. (   ) Which of the following is NOT one of the Gates Foundation's causes?
    (A) Trying to stop the spread of diseases
    (B) Helping people in poor countries
    (C) Assisting employees of Microsoft
    (D) Improving the services of libraries

5. (   ) What does the article imply about billionaires?
    (A) Some of them are concerned with the *Forbes* list.
    (B) Most of them plan to give all their money away.
    (C) Many of them plan to donate to the Gates Foundation.
    (D) All of them easily made their fortunes.

Writing about the Article
Answer each question based on the article.

1. How did John D. Rockefeller donate his money?
    He gave it to _____.

2. Why did Warren Buffet give so much money to the Gates Foundation?
    He admired _____.

3. How often does *Forbes* publish its list of the world's richest people?
    The list is published _____.

Vocabulary Building
Choose the best word to fill in each blank.

1. I _____ Mr. Fieldman, one of the best teachers in our school.
   (A) appear   (B) donate   (C) connect   (D) admire

2. With this vacation package, you have the _____ of staying in a 4 or 5 star hotel.
   (A) action   (B) option   (C) concern   (D) plan

3. In poor countries, _____ are often spread through dirty food and water.
   (A) diseases   (B) lists   (C) doubts   (D) foundations

4. Paul is very _____, but all of his money came from his father.
   (A) recent   (B) wealthy   (C) incredible   (D) expensive

5. I'm worried about the environment. I _____ money every month to a group that plants trees.
   (A) put   (B) earn   (C) work   (D) donate

6. Many people send their children to schools overseas. It's a growing _____.
   (A) member   (B) magazine   (C) trend   (D) fortune

7. The _____ builds houses for poor people across the country.
   (A) charity   (B) library   (C) century   (D) Internet

8. What time are they going to _____ the winner of the contest?
   (A) appear   (B) announce   (C) spend   (D) start

Phrase Building
Write the correct phrase in each blank.

● give away   ● hold onto   ● put out   ● turn around

By the time they graduate from university, most students have a large number of books. Many students _____ them, to add to a home library. Others _____ the books that they don't want anymore. Charities welcome this kind of donation. They sell the books to raise money for a cause. With just a small amount of money, a charity can feed a poor child or give him or her medicine. That action may help _____ the child's condition and offer hope for the future.

Grammar Exercise

Adjective Clauses

Fill in each blank with *who, which,* **or** *where.*

Example: My car is the one _____ is parked by the tree.
Answer: My car is the one *which* is parked by the tree.

1. Harry is the friend _____ is helping me move.

2. Is this the place _____ the party will be held?

3. All of the bags _____ were left outside got wet.

4. The building _____ my father owns is downtown.

5. Our company is looking for someone _____ can speak French.

Listening Exercise   Track 32

Listen to the conversation. Then, answer the following questions.

1. (   ) What are the people discussing?
   (A) Ways to make more money
   (B) A very lucky bus driver
   (C) The best place for a holiday
   (D) How wealth changes our lives

2. (   ) How many years did Mr. Grant buy lottery tickets?
   (A) 5
   (B) 10
   (C) 15
   (D) 25

3. (   ) What does Mr. Grant plan to do?
   (A) Go into another line of work
   (B) Quit his job immediately
   (C) Continue his life as before
   (D) Take a very long vacation

Listening Activity 🔘 Track 33

Listen to the report. Then, fill in the information in the chart.

1. What type of building were people raising money for?	
2. What was the problem with the building?	
3. How many people donated things?	
4. How much money did they raise?	
5. How much money did the city add?	

Discussion Questions

1. What charities are big in your country? What do they do?

2. If you aren't able to donate money to a charity, what are some other ways you can help them?

3. Do rich people have a responsibility to give away some of their money? Why or why not?

Discussion Activity

Imagine you have one billion dollars to give away. Where will the money go? Working with several classmates, make a plan for spending the money. Write down three groups or causes that you would like to donate to, and decide how much money each one will get. When you are finished, compare the list to those of other classmates.

Example: $200 million should go to the Red Cross. They help many people after natural disasters like earthquakes....

Computer Actors 12

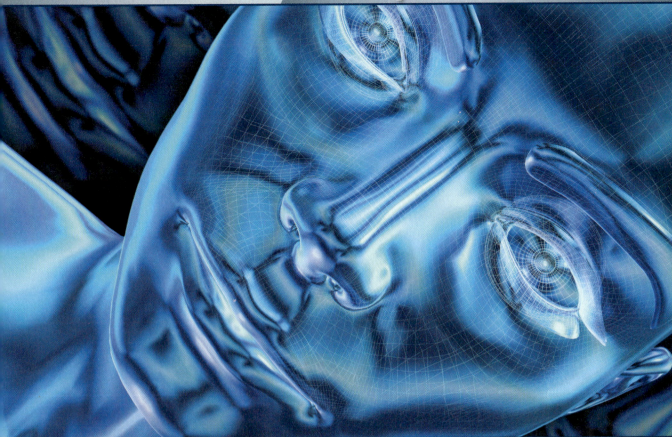

Pre-Reading Questions
Discuss these questions in pairs.

1. How often do you go out to the movies?

2. What's your favorite way to watch a movie? (at a theater? on DVD?)

3. What are some movies with good special effects?

Consider the Topic
Read each statement. Check if you agree or disagree with it.

	agree	disagree
1. I like movies with 3D characters.	☐	☐
2. I love watching cartoons.	☐	☐
3. Soon, all movies will be made by computers, and there will be few real actors left.	☐	☐

67

Reading Passage   Track 34

1   While watching movies, it's getting hard to tell what is and isn't real. Thanks to computers, movie makers can now use their full **imaginations**. There's even a new type of **character** – made **entirely** by computers – which is getting more and more screen time.

5   Making the impossible look easy has always been a part of movie magic. **As far back as** 1895, filmmakers used special effects in movies. Over the years, many new techniques were developed. Then, starting in the 1970s, computers took their place at the center of the **process**.

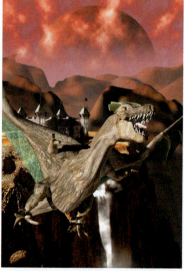

One of the first movies to widely use 3D
10   computer generated imagery (CGI) was *Tron* (1982). In the **following** years, more CGI characters were brought to life, **one by one**. Then, *Jurassic Park* (1993) brought us an island full of man-eating dinosaurs. Shortly afterwards,
15   *Toy Story* (1995) became the first cartoon made entirely with 3D CGI effects. It was a big hit, and audiences loved the characters.

By using "motion capture" technology, filmmakers can make the movements of CGI
20   humans even more lifelike. With this technique, a real actor wears sensors on his face and body. The sensors record the actor's **movements** and send the information to a computer. Then, the movements are given to a CGI character. This technique was used to make the creature Gollum in the second and third *The Lord of the Rings* movies (2002, 2003). Other films, like *Beowulf* (2007), have
25   also used motion capture to help create CGI humans.

It is still **rather** easy to tell that a CGI human is not real. But the technology is improving every year. Over time, many problems (like the teeth and eyes looking **fake**) will be solved. We will certainly see more CGI animals, monsters, and people in movies and TV shows. The question is – in the future,
30   how many real actors will be put **out of work** by computer actors?

---

[7] technique – method/way of doing something
[10] generated – made/created
[17] audience – group of people who watch something

[20] human – person
[20] sensor – information detector
[23] creature – living thing

Questions about the Reading   Choose the best answer.

1. (   ) What is the main idea?
   (A) *Tron* was important in the history of CGI films.
   (B) Many people go to the movies to see incredible special effects.
   (C) More and more film characters are being made by computers.
   (D) All the humans in *Beowulf* were CGI characters.

2. (   ) In what year was a film made with many CGI dinosaurs?
   (A) 1895
   (B) 1982
   (C) 1993
   (D) 2003

3. (   ) What was special about Gollum?
   (A) Motion capture was used to help make the character.
   (B) Gollum had an important role in a CGI cartoon.
   (C) He was the only CGI character in *The Lord of the Rings*.
   (D) Little money was spent to bring the creature to life.

4. (   ) According to the article, what is a problem with using CGI?
   (A) Actors say it is making them lose work.
   (B) Some human body parts made with CGI don't look real.
   (C) It's very difficult to make CGI monsters.
   (D) Only the world's fastest computers can create CGI effects.

5. (   ) What does the word *hit* in line 16 mean?
   (A) attack
   (B) shot
   (C) success
   (D) try

Writing about the Article   Answer each question based on the article.

1. When did computers become important in movie making?

   That started happening _____ .

2. How are an actor's movements recorded during the motion capture process?

   They are recorded _____ .

3. What problems do CGI human characters have?

   The characters' _____ .

Vocabulary Building Choose the best word to fill in each blank.

1. The watch looks _____. I don't think you should buy it.
   (A) full   (B) fake   (C) special   (D) hard

2. Buying a house is a long _____. It can take months.
   (A) process   (B) question   (C) technique   (D) effect

3. Don't make any quick _____. That dog looks dangerous!
   (A) movements (B) problems   (C) types   (D) people

4. Who was your favorite _____ in the film? Mine was the hero.
   (A) movie   (B) computer   (C) future   (D) character

5. The book was good, but it was _____ long.
   (A) rather   (B) over   (C) every   (D) while

6. The card is made _____ of dark chocolate. After you read it, you can eat it!
   (A) likely   (B) usually   (C) entirely   (D) widely

7. This week, we talked about dramas. In the _____ class, we'll discuss action films.
   (A) full   (B) following   (C) every   (D) real

8. The teacher told me to use my _____. So, I drew myself flying.
   (A) actor   (B) information   (C) human   (D) imagination

Phrase Building Write the correct phrase in each blank.

● one by one   ● out of work   ● as far back as   ● take one's place

People have taken their families to watch films at the Paradise Theater since _____ 1930. It's one of Lakeville's oldest buildings. Unfortunately, the Paradise is starting to look and feel old-fashioned. _____, people are taking their business to modern theaters like the Lakeville Cineplex. Because of the slowdown in ticket sales, many Paradise employees are _____. The theater's owner is looking for ways to save the business. One idea is to show older movies and cartoons.

Grammar Exercise

The Passive Voice

Change each sentence into the passive form.

Example: She wrote the book in 1997.
Answer: *The book was written by her in 1997.*

1. The dog ate all the food.

   _____.

2. Tired drivers cause many accidents.

   _____.

3. A strong wind blew the sign down.

   _____.

4. The children made a lot of noise.

   _____.

5. Two companies control the market.

   _____.

Listening Exercise   Track 35

Listen to the conversation. Then, answer the following questions.

1. (   ) What does the woman think about the computer actor?
    (A) He wasn't at all believable.
    (B) He was unnecessary.
    (C) He looked mostly realistic.
    (D) He had a good voice.

2. (   ) What did the CGI character do?
    (A) He jumped very high.
    (B) He married a model.
    (C) He became really tall.
    (D) He caused a problem.

3. (   ) What did the woman dislike about the character?
    (A) The voice
    (B) The mouth
    (C) The eyes
    (D) The skin

71

Listening Activity Track 36

Listen to the report. Then, fill in the information in the chart.

1. What are the actors worried about losing?	
2. What does the group call itself?	
3. What does the group ask people not to do?	
4. What percentage of films contain some CGI?	
5. When may that number grow to 50%?	

Discussion Questions

1. We've seen many movies about monsters and magic, police officers and politicians. What kinds of movies would you like to see more of?

2. CGI characters are already replacing some people in movies. What are some other fields in which CGI people (or robots) might take jobs away from people?

3. Soon, people may have CGI friends on their computers, similar to CGI movie characters. How would you like to have a CGI friend?

Discussion Activity

Hold a mini debate. On one side are filmmakers who support making more CGI movies. On the other side are actors who don't want to see any more CGI humans. First, divide into small groups and decide who will be on each side. Then, come up with a few reasons for your side's position. Finally, hold the mini debate.

Example: We are on the side of movie makers. We think movies are made for movie watchers, not for actors. If the audience wants to see more CGI humans, then that's what we'll give them....

Pre-Reading Questions

Discuss these questions in pairs.

1. How many people live in your town or city?

2. What do visitors to your hometown like to see?

3. What is New York City famous for?

Consider the Topic

Read each statement. Check if you agree or disagree with it.

	agree	disagree
1. New York City would be a fun place to visit.	☐	☐
2. I like going to museums and art galleries.	☐	☐
3. I don't mind spending a lot on hotel rooms.	☐	☐

1 New York City has a special **personality**. It's the home of thousands of artists, singers, and celebrities, from a wide **variety** of **backgrounds**. Tourists travel
5 there in large numbers to enjoy an amazing number of sights and sounds. With so much to offer, it's easy to see why the city's nickname is the Big Apple.

10 New York City has long had an important place in American history. For millions of immigrants in the 19th and 20th centuries, it was their point of entry into the USA. **Greeting** them was the Statue of Liberty, a gift from France to the USA in 1886. The city is also the home of the United Nations, the New York Stock Exchange, and the offices of many **international** companies.

15 The city is **made up of** five sections, or "boroughs": Manhattan, Brooklyn, Queens, the Bronx, and Staten Island. Although the city is **spread out**, its eight million plus residents can easily **get around** on the excellent subway system. Each year, more than 1.5 billion riders travel on one of 26 routes.

There is certainly a lot to see, which is why more than 40 million tourists
20 travel to the city every year. People love visiting the Empire State Building, Central Park, and Rockefeller Center. Plus, there are great museums like the Met and MoMA. **Attending** shows on Broadway, concerts at Lincoln Center, and events at smaller theaters is also popular with locals and tourists.

Many of these activities are expensive, as are hotels. Spending $300 per night
25 in Manhattan is common. However, one of the best things about New York City is free – walking around interesting **neighborhoods** like Greenwich Village and Chinatown. Each one has its own character, but they have one thing in common. Though their residents may come from many countries and cultures, they're all **proud** to call themselves New Yorkers.

---

11 immigrant – person who settles in a new country
14 New York Stock Exchange – place where stocks are bought and sold
22 Met – Metropolitan Museum of Art
22 MoMA - Museum of Modern Art

Questions about the Reading

Choose the best answer.

1. ( ) According to the article, why does the city deserve its nickname?
    (A) There is a lot to see and do there.
    (B) Residents enjoy eating fruit.
    (C) It is the world's largest city.
    (D) New York City has great weather.

2. ( ) Many immigrants entered the USA through New York City. What idea does this fact support?
    (A) The city is important in US history.
    (B) Tourists love to visit New York City.
    (C) The Statue of Liberty was a gift.
    (D) Many companies have offices there.

3. ( ) What is true about New York City's boroughs?
    (A) They're all exactly the same size.
    (B) It's easy to travel from one to another.
    (C) They are the home of 1.5 billion people.
    (D) More are added to the city every year.

4. ( ) How many subway lines does the city have?
    (A) 5
    (B) 8
    (C) 15
    (D) 26

5. ( ) What is the cheapest thing about New York City?
    (A) Hotel rates
    (B) Broadway shows
    (C) Neighborhood tours
    (D) Theater tickets

Writing about the Article

Answer each question based on the article.

1. How did the USA get the Statue of Liberty?

   It was given _____ .

2. Where can people attend shows or other events?

   They can go _____ .

3. What is the problem with hotels in the city?

   They often _____ .

Vocabulary Building   Choose the best word to fill in each blank.

1. I grew up in this _____. It sure has changed a lot since I moved away.
   (A) museum   (B) character   (C) neighborhood   (D) tourist

2. We want our son and daughter to _____ this high school. It's the best in the city.
   (A) attend   (B) travel   (C) greet   (D) offer

3. My university has a few _____ students. Two of them are from England.
   (A) expensive   (B) free   (C) own   (D) international

4. I'm very _____ of my sister. She owns her own company.
   (A) proud   (B) amazing   (C) common   (D) easy

5. Cathy works as a salesperson, but her _____ is in web design.
   (A) theater   (B) background   (C) nickname   (D) system

6. They've got a great _____ of jackets. It's too bad none of them are my size.
   (A) company   (B) culture   (C) variety   (D) entry

7. We'll be at the airport to _____ you when you arrive.
   (A) greet   (B) offer   (C) spend   (D) walk

8. Felicia doesn't talk a lot. It's just her _____.
   (A) resident   (B) route   (C) personality   (D) activity

Phrase Building   Write the correct phrase in each blank.

● come from   ● get around   ● made up of   ● spread out

This industrial park is _____ 47 buildings. It's the largest such complex in the country. Actually, it's almost like its own city. We've got restaurants, convenience stores, and even a small hospital. The buildings are _____ over a large area, so it takes a long time to walk from end to end. Most people _____ on the shuttle bus. It runs from 5:00 AM to 8:00 PM. Another option is to ride a bicycle. There are bike lanes on every street.

Grammar Exercise

Quantifiers

Choose the correct word to complete each sentence.

Example: We don't have (much/many) time, so let's hurry.
Answer: We don't have (much)/many) time, so let's hurry.

1. There are still (lot/many) forms left to fill out.

2. (Some/Much) of the items are already sold out.

3. (Few/Little) people work in this building.

4. Is there (much/many) more to do? It's getting late.

5. I come here once a month. (Most/Lot) days, I work at the main office.

Listening Exercise   Track 38

Listen to the conversation. Then, answer the following questions.

1. (   ) Who are the people?
   (A) Tour guides
   (B) Immigrants
   (C) City workers
   (D) Tourists

2. (   ) What did the people see first?
   (A) The Empire State Building
   (B) Central Park
   (C) The MoMA
   (D) A Greek neighborhood

3. (   ) How will the people get to the restaurant?
   (A) Via taxi
   (B) By horse
   (C) On foot
   (D) By bus

Listening Activity Track 39

Listen to the report. Then, fill in the information in the chart.

1. What can people read to get event information?	
2. Name three types of events that are listed.	
3. What basic information is given?	
4. What else might a listing tell people?	
5. What's another way to get information?	

Discussion Questions

1. If you could travel to New York City, what would you like to see and do there?

2. New York City is expensive, yet it attracts many tourists. Is it worth it to spend a month's salary (or more) on a short vacation? Why or why not?

3. Many cities like New York are getting bigger and bigger. At the same time, more people are leaving the countryside and small towns. What is good and bad about this situation?

Discussion Activity

A visitor from New York is traveling to your city. Plan two days of cultural events. First, think about the interesting places that your guest can visit during the day. Then, consider some good evening activities. Finally, choose the best ones and plan a schedule!

Example: Our city has three famous museums, but our friend would probably like the National Art Gallery. So that will be the first place we visit....

Pre-Reading Questions
Discuss these questions in pairs.

1. What do people use water for every day?

2. Where does fresh water come from? (lakes? rivers?)

3. Are there many polluted rivers and lakes in your country?

Consider the Topic
Read each statement. Check if you agree or disagree with it.

	agree	disagree
1. My monthly water bills are very low.	☐	☐
2. I am careful about not wasting water.	☐	☐
3. Without clean water, it would be hard to live.	☐	☐

Reading Passage 🔘 Track 40

1   Water is our most important natural resource. Yet, although it covers most of the world, only 2.5% of it is salt free. Demand for fresh water has risen **sharply** in the last 50 years, and it is still rising. That's already causing serious problems. Finding all the answers may be one of the biggest

5   challenges of the 21st century.

   There are several reasons behind the growing **crisis**. The first is waste. About 70% of our fresh water is used to grow crops. It takes 1,000 tons of water to grow just one ton of wheat. Unfortunately, around 60% of that water is **wasted**. Better irrigation methods would help the **situation**.

10   Pollution is another big problem. Many of the world's great rivers, such as the Ganges in India, are badly polluted. Yet, 350 million people **rely on** the Ganges. Their **health** is **affected** by the health of the river. Steps are being taken to clean up some rivers, but it is expensive and can take many years.

   Overuse also **puts pressure on** water supplies. In the USA, 95% of the

15   country's fresh water comes from underground sources. Levels are quickly falling, since so much water is used to grow crops and raise livestock. Once used, those **supplies** are gone forever, since they are not refilled by rainwater. The key there is to lower demand.

In many places around the world, people

20 already live in crisis. More than one billion people have no access to clean water. That leads to millions of deaths every year, including thousands of children dying every day in Africa. By 2025, **as many as** 25 African

25 countries may face water shortages. It could even lead to wars over water rights.

   The fresh water crisis is not **limited** to poor countries. Indeed, rich and poor countries from Asia to Europe to North America are facing shortages. It's a growing problem that could soon affect us all.

---

² demand – need   ¹⁶ livestock – farm animals
⁷ ton – 2,000 pounds (907 kg)   ²¹ access – way or chance to use
⁹ irrigation – watering crops   ²⁵ shortage – lack of

Questions about the Reading

Choose the best answer.

1. (   ) What is the main idea?
    (A) The lack of fresh water is a problem that keeps getting bigger.
    (B) There should be laws against wasting water.
    (C) Wheat uses more fresh water than any other crop.
    (D) In India, the Ganges is a source of water for 350 million people.

2. (   ) What does the article suggest about salt water?
    (A) It is used to water crops.
    (B) It makes up almost all of the Earth's water.
    (C) It is in high demand.
    (D) It has become a problem in the last 50 years.

3. (   ) What percentage of the world's fresh water is used for growing food?
    (A) 2.5%
    (B) 60%
    (C) 70%
    (D) 95%

4. (   ) What is the problem with cleaning up rivers?
    (A) It costs a lot of money.
    (B) It is hard to see the benefit.
    (C) It has few people's support.
    (D) It may not be legal.

5. (   ) Which of the following is true?
    (A) Every African country has serious water shortages.
    (B) Not only poor countries are facing water problems.
    (C) The world's fresh water crisis isn't spreading yet.
    (D) It is possible to refill underground water supplies.

Writing about the Article

Answer each question based on the article.

1. How much water is needed to grow one ton of wheat?

    It takes _____ .

2. How much of the USA's fresh water comes from underground supplies?

    In the USA, _____ .

3. What might African countries fight over in the future?

    They might fight _____ .

Vocabulary Building Choose the best word to fill in each blank.

1. I try not to _____ paper. I only print things out when necessary.
   (A) cover   (B) affect   (C) cause   (D) waste

2. It's a difficult _____, but it will get better over time.
   (A) situation   (B) reason   (C) source   (D) health

3. Recently, land prices have fallen _____. It may be a good time to buy property.
   (A) still   (B) yet   (C) since   (D) sharply

4. High raw material costs are strongly _____ the housing industry.
   (A) lowering   (B) growing   (C) dying   (D) affecting

5. With three fires burning at the same time, the area faced a _____.
   (A) crisis   (B) method   (C) demand   (D) world

6. We have enough _____ for another two months. After that, we'll need to buy more canned food and medicine.
   (A) answers   (B) challenges   (C) supplies   (D) shortages

7. Space is _____, so we'll have to put your desk in the corner.
   (A) fresh   (B) serious   (C) limited   (D) natural

8. To stay in good _____, you should exercise often and eat well.
   (A) health   (B) pressure   (C) access   (D) crisis

Phrase Building Write the correct phrase in each blank.

● lead to   ● rely on   ● put pressure on   ● as many as

In the village of Logana, there is only one well. _____ 500 people use it every day. They _____ it for fresh water for drinking and cooking. Often, the water runs out, leading to serious problems. To discuss ways to solve the crisis, the villagers held a meeting. They agreed to _____ the village leaders to dig another well. Even better, they could lay down a pipe from Ikana Lake to Logana. That would supply them with plenty of water.

Grammar Exercise

Word Form

Write the correct form of the word in parentheses.

Example: Air (pollute) _____ is a big problem in the city.
Answer: Air *pollution* is a big problem in the city.

1. I will (serious) _____ consider your request. You'll have my answer soon.

2. Our traffic problem is (limit) _____ to the downtown area.

3. Last winter, snow (cover) _____ the entire field.

4. School bus (drive) _____ have a lot of responsibility.

5. Children don't like (clean) _____ their rooms, but it is necessary.

Listening Exercise Track 41

Listen to the conversation. Then, answer the following questions.

1. (   ) When is the last time it rained?
   (A) Three days ago
   (B) Five days ago
   (C) One week ago
   (D) One month ago

2. (   ) What does the man no longer do?
   (A) Drive to work
   (B) Take showers
   (C) Wash his car
   (D) Grow vegetables

3. (   ) What will probably happen soon?
   (A) Heavy rains will come.
   (B) The price of food will increase.
   (C) Farmers will start dying.
   (D) The woman's salary will go up.

Listening Activity   Track 42

Listen to the report. Then, fill in the information in the chart.

1. How long have people complained about the problem?	
2. Who made the announcement?	
3. What will be cleaned up?	
4. How long will it take?	
5. What will not be allowed during the cleanup?	

Discussion Questions

1. Has your country ever faced a water shortage? How long did it last? How did it finally end?

2. What can you do in your daily life to reduce your water usage?

3. Do you feel mostly positive or negative about the future? Will countries find a way to overcome their water problems?

Discussion Activity

Imagine your country is facing a water shortage. Come up with a plan to deal with it. Decide what the people, government, and businesses should do. Also, decide what should happen to those who don't follow the new plan (such as businesses who continue using too much water).

Example: First, we need to explain to everyone that there is a serious problem. We will give people a list of suggestions about how to save water. For example...

Discuss these questions in pairs.

1. Do you like any singers or bands from other countries?

2. Do you like to eat at any international restaurants? (Ex: Italian? Indian?)

3. How can people learn about new overseas fashion styles?

Consider the Topic Read each statement. Check if you agree or disagree with it.

	agree	disagree
1. I like watching foreign TV shows.	☐	☐
2. It's interesting to read books from other countries.	☐	☐
3. Younger people are more interested in foreign cultures than older people.	☐	☐

Reading Passage   Track 43

1   With the growth of the Internet, tourism, and the global economy, it feels like the world is getting smaller. Ideas, products, and **customs** are flying from country to country. As the number of cultural **exports** grows, the world is truly becoming a global village.

5   Entertainment is one of the most popular cultural exports. Every year, movies from Hollywood are watched by billions of people worldwide. **Likewise**, TV shows and music are **making their way** from America to Asia. As people enjoy these
10   entertainment products, they also learn about the ideas and values of other cultures.

Books can give an even deeper insight into a foreign country's history and beliefs. Novels from South America, Asia, and elsewhere have been **translated**
15   into many languages. For younger readers, the Harry Potter novels (from England) and comics from Japan are examples of very successful exports.

Food is a tasty way for the world's cultures to **meet up**. For more than 100 years, Chinese immigrants have opened restaurants from London to Rio. Likewise, Indian and Arabic food can be found in most major cities. When we
20   eat at these places, new words like "nan" and "falafel" enter our vocabulary. Then, of course, there's fast food. Though **unhealthy**, it certainly is popular.

Fashion is another big cultural export. In the past, it took months for trends to spread to nearby countries. With the Internet, a new style from Paris can become famous overnight. Plus, fast shipping means a shop in South Africa
25   can receive French goods **in no time**.

Some people are unhappy about the **rapid** spread of foreign cultures. They worry it will **harm** their local identity. For sure, young people are often interested in new ideas and products from **abroad**. Yet, the more we learn about each other, the closer we become. That helps export our most important
30   cultural products: greater understanding and world peace.

---

¹² insight – knowledge/understanding   ²⁰ falafel – fried ball made of peas and spices
²⁰ nan – a kind of bread   ²⁷ identity – feeling of who you are

Questions about the Reading
Choose the best answer.

1. (   ) What is the main idea?
   - (A) Because of the Internet, information spreads very quickly.
   - (B) It's expensive to ship products from one country to another.
   - (C) Many cities have Chinese, Arabic, and Indian restaurants.
   - (D) In many ways, our lives are influenced by the world's cultures.

2. (   ) According to the article, what is one way we learn foreign words?
   - (A) By shopping on the Internet
   - (B) By translating books
   - (C) By watching movies
   - (D) By eating at restaurants

3. (   ) What cultural product is NOT discussed in the article?
   - (A) Movies
   - (B) Food
   - (C) Art
   - (D) Clothes

4. (   ) What does the word *values* in line 11 mean?
   - (A) things held in importance
   - (B) considerations of price
   - (C) questions of worth
   - (D) matters of usefulness

5. (   ) What does the article imply about the spread of fashion?
   - (A) In previous years, new styles spread more slowly than music.
   - (B) Things used to take a lot longer than they do now.
   - (C) Goods from Europe once had the largest market.
   - (D) Before the Net, it was impossible for fashions to spread worldwide.

Writing about the Article
Answer each question based on the article.

1. Where do a lot of popular movies come from?

   Many popular movies _____ .

2. What can people learn by reading books from other countries?

   People can learn _____ .

3. What kinds of restaurants are found in many cities?

   There are _____ .

Vocabulary Building — Choose the best word to fill in each blank.

1. Due to a _____ increase in steel prices, construction costs have gone up.
   (A) rapid   (B) cultural   (C) deep   (D) close

2. Fruit is one of our biggest _____. We sell fruit to more than 100 countries worldwide.
   (A) exports   (B) styles   (C) restaurants   (D) ideas

3. If you stay in the sun too long, it could _____ your skin.
   (A) spread   (B) receive   (C) harm   (D) seem

4. I'm a computer programmer. _____, my brother is a computer expert.
   (A) Then   (B) Likewise   (C) While   (D) When

5. Some of my friends want to study _____. One is already in Germany.
   (A) worldwide   (B) country   (C) abroad   (D) foreign

6. In many countries, it is a _____ to exchange gifts during Christmas.
   (A) product   (B) custom   (C) shop   (D) culture

7. Eating too much sugar is _____. The same goes for junk food.
   (A) local   (B) unhealthy   (C) famous   (D) close

8. Can you help me _____ this poster? I can't read Spanish.
   (A) translate   (B) mean   (C) enjoy   (D) become

Phrase Building — Write the correct phrase in each blank. (Remember to use the correct word form.)

● meet up   ● make one's way   ● as well as   ● in no time

Next week, Larry, Bill, and I will go camping together. We all live in different cities, so each person will _____ to the campground by himself. The plan is to _____ at 11:00 AM. After setting up our tents and other equipment, we'll have lunch. Then, people can swim, hike, or do whatever they like. Fortunately, I go camping a lot, so I can put up a tent _____. I want to spend the whole afternoon in the lake!

Grammar Exercise

Every, Any, and All

Fill in each blank with *every*, *any*, **or** *all*.

Example: _____ of the money is right here, in my hand.
Answer: *All* of the money is right here, in my hand.

1. We wake up at 7:30 AM _____ day.

2. I didn't understand _____ of the movie. It was in Dutch, and I don't speak a word of the language!

3. _____ student in the class has his or her own notebook computer.

4. During the storm, _____ of the windows were broken.

5. Is there _____ salt left, or should I get some at the store?

Listening Exercise   Track 44

Listen to the conversation. Then, answer the following questions.

1. (   ) When does the movie's story take place?
    (A) In the past
    (B) In the present
    (C) In the future
    (D) In several time periods

2. (   ) What did the man do in college?
    (A) He saw a French movie.
    (B) He studied French cooking.
    (C) He learned some French.
    (D) He traveled to France.

3. (   ) What will the woman do first?
    (A) Go to a store
    (B) Get something to eat
    (C) Meet another friend
    (D) See the movie

Listening Activity 🔘 Track 45

Listen to the report. Then, fill in the information in the chart.

1. When will the activity be held?	
2. Where will it be held?	
3. How many countries will have booths?	
4. What kinds of things will they show?	
5. What will take place on the stage?	

Discussion Questions

1. What cultural products from your country are popular overseas?

2. Do people spend too much time learning about foreign cultures? Should they spend more time learning about their own culture?

3. People are talking about the spread of a "global culture." In the future, do you think everyone in the world will share the same culture? Why or why not?

Discussion Activity

Working with a few classmates, make a short ad for a cultural product from your country. It can be for a new movie, a food product, an item of clothing, or something else. After you decide on the item, put together an ad. (It can be as short as 20-30 seconds long.) When you're finished, try it out on your classmates!

Example: Have you ever tried dried tofu? It's a delicious snack that you can enjoy any time of the day....

Pre-Reading Questions

Discuss these questions in pairs.

1. At what age do people usually retire?

2. In your country, is the average population age going up?

3. Is the number of young people rising or falling?

Consider the Topic

Read each statement. Check if you agree or disagree with it.

	agree	disagree
1. At least one of my relatives is older than 70.	☐	☐
2. I only want to have one child.	☐	☐
3. I would like to live to be 100.	☐	☐

Reading Passage 🖸 Track 46

1 Many countries are going through an important population shift. People are having fewer children, and lifespans are getting longer. The result is an average population age that keeps going up. The situation is creating some serious problems.

5 Falling fertility rates are the first key to the **issue**. In most developed countries, the rate has fallen in the last 50 years. For example, in Japan, it went from 2.00 in 1960 to 1.32 in 2006. Taiwan's rate fell from around 5.00 in 1960 to 1.12 in 2006. To keep its population **stable**, a country needs a fertility rate of 2.10.

Longer lifespans are the second key. With better healthcare and **nutrition**, 10 we're living longer than ever. For example, in 2004, the **average** lifespan in Brazil was 76 years for women and 68 for men. In Egypt, the average that year was 73 for women and 69 for men. These numbers are climbing and could **reach** 100 in the coming decades.

Living longer is great, but it leads to some problems. After people **retire**, they 15 collect pensions, and their healthcare costs go up. Much of the burden for paying these costs **falls on** the current workforce. Yet, as the workforce gets smaller (**due to** low fertility rates), less tax money is collected. The situation puts heavy pressure on companies and governments.

To turn things around, some governments are **encouraging** 20 people to have more children. Robots are being built to work in offices and provide healthcare. And, through immigration, countries like England and the USA are adding to their workforce.

Some countries are **in a rush** to find answers. In Japan, more 25 than 20% of the population is 65 or older. That will probably climb to over 30% by 2030. Other countries, like Germany and Italy, are facing **similar** situations. Time will tell which methods can successfully deal with our aging populations.

---

[2] lifespan – number of years that a person lives
[5] fertility rate – average number of children that a woman has
[5] developed country – modern/advanced country
[15] pension – money received from one's job after retiring
[15] burden – responsibility/trouble
[16] workforce – working population

Questions about the Reading

Choose the best answer.

1. (   ) What fertility rate leads to a stable population?
   - (A) 1.12
   - (B) 1.32
   - (C) 2.10
   - (D) 5.00

2. (   ) What does the article suggest about better nutrition?
   - (A) It is the cause of high healthcare costs.
   - (B) It is related to falling fertility rates.
   - (C) It has little to do with aging populations.
   - (D) It is one reason for our longer lifespans.

3. (   ) What was the average lifespan for Egyptian men in 2004?
   - (A) 68
   - (B) 69
   - (C) 73
   - (D) 76

4. (   ) What is NOT a problem with people living longer?
   - (A) A lack of interesting things to do
   - (B) A smaller tax base
   - (C) A heavier pressure on the workforce
   - (D) A rise in healthcare costs

5. (   ) How is England increasing its number of workers?
   - (A) By encouraging people to retire earlier
   - (B) By providing better healthcare
   - (C) By letting people in from other countries
   - (D) By building worker robots

Writing about the Article

Answer each question based on the article.

1. What was Japan's fertility rate in 2006?

   That year, _____ .

2. When was the average lifespan 76 for Brazilian women?

   The average was _____ .

3. What problem is Italy facing?

   Much of the population _____ .

Vocabulary Building   Choose the best word to fill in each blank.

1. What is the _____ age of the club's members?
   (A) average   (B) serious   (C) interesting   (D) heavy

2. After my father _____, he plans to move to the countryside.
   (A) climbs   (B) collects   (C) retires   (D) rises

3. Global warming is an important _____. We have to work together to
   deal with it.
   (A) issue   (B) country   (C) decade   (D) population

4. Both shirts are very _____. They look almost exactly the same.
   (A) important   (B) current   (C) successful   (D) similar

5. France's population _____ 60 million several years ago.
   (A) reached   (B) collected   (C) provided   (D) built

6. Between 70 and 75 people eat here every night. The number is _____.
   (A) first   (B) expensive   (C) stable   (D) long

7. A child needs good _____ to grow up strong and healthy.
   (A) nutrition   (B) government   (C) population   (D) office

8. It's a great book. I would _____ you to read it.
   (A) lead   (B) rise   (C) start   (D) encourage

Phrase Building   Write the correct phrase in each blank. (Remember to use the correct word form.)

● due to   ● fall on   ● in a rush   ● turn around

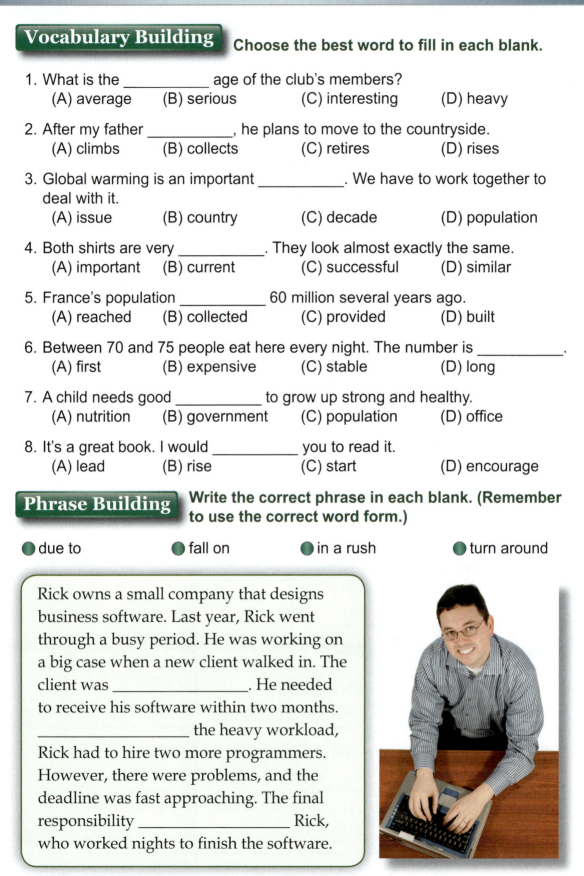

Rick owns a small company that designs
business software. Last year, Rick went
through a busy period. He was working on
a big case when a new client walked in. The
client was _____. He needed
to receive his software within two months.
_____ the heavy workload,
Rick had to hire two more programmers.
However, there were problems, and the
deadline was fast approaching. The final
responsibility _____ Rick,
who worked nights to finish the software.

Grammar Exercise

To, For, and With

Fill in each blank with *to*, *for*, **or** *with*.

Example: _____ better understand the problem, Ms. Kim visited the factory herself.

Answer: *To* better understand the problem, Ms. Kim visited the factory herself.

1. Thank you _____ letting me know about the situation.

2. I have no problem _____ employees trying things their own way.

3. Here's the payment _____ the work that you did.

4. It takes a long time _____ train someone new.

5. _____ a rising crime rate, the city is becoming very dangerous.

Listening Exercise   Track 47

Listen to the conversation. Then, answer the following questions.

1. (   ) What is the woman considering doing?
    (A) Writing a field report
    (B) Working as a nurse
    (C) Getting better healthcare
    (D) Going on vacation

2. (   ) What does the man have trouble believing?
    (A) That the healthcare field is growing
    (B) That the job market is bad
    (C) That the population may be aging
    (D) That the woman is wrong

3. (   ) What do the woman and her mother have in common?
    (A) Health issues
    (B) Career interests
    (C) Money problems
    (D) Education levels

Listening Activity 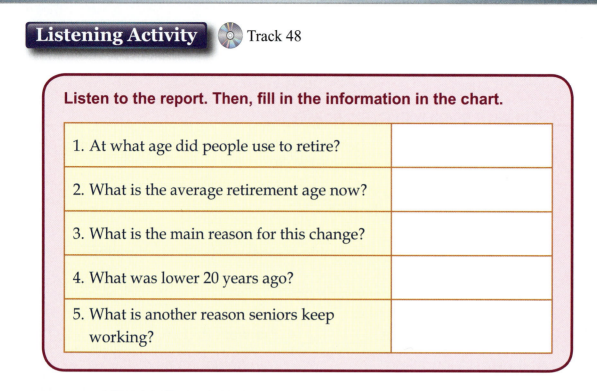 Track 48

Listen to the report. Then, fill in the information in the chart.

1. At what age did people use to retire?	
2. What is the average retirement age now?	
3. What is the main reason for this change?	
4. What was lower 20 years ago?	
5. What is another reason seniors keep working?	

Discussion Questions

1. At what age would you like to retire? What would you like to do during your retirement?

2. Do you often see older people (over 65 years old) working? What kinds of jobs do they do?

3. Is an aging population nothing but a problem? Or, do you see anything good coming from it? If so, what?

Discussion Activity

Imagine your country's fertility rate is falling, yet the average population age is rising. Make an action plan to address the situation. Will you encourage people to have more children? Will you raise the average retirement age? Will you let more people immigrate to your country? Or, do you have some other ideas?

Example: Immigration is the key to solving this problem. We can let in very skilled people. That will help our economy and increase the amount of taxes collected....

Discuss these questions in pairs.

1. Have you ever visited www.youtube.com?

2. What kinds of videos do people upload to the Internet?

3. Where do you usually get your news? (newspaper? TV?)

Consider the Topic Read each statement. Check if you agree or disagree with it.

	agree	disagree
1. It's easy to film a video and upload it to the Internet.	☐	☐
2. I like to watch funny videos online.	☐	☐
3. I often send my friends links to good websites.	☐	☐

Reading Passage 🔘 Track 49

1 Since the Internet's growth in the 1990s, people have expected the Net
   to change the world. But how? Already, e-mail has changed the way we
   communicate, and online shopping has become an important sales channel.
   Now, online videos are affecting the way people get news and **express**
5 themselves. The leader in this information shift is YouTube.

   YouTube opened its online doors in December 2005, as an easy way for
   people to share videos. The **response** was incredible. The site quickly became
   the home of millions of home videos, music videos, TV clips, and more. Now,
   more than 100 million videos are viewed every day! Google felt so strongly
10 about YouTube that it bought the company for $1.65 billion in 2006.

   One sign of YouTube's growing power is its **influence** on politics. During the
   2008 US presidential **election**, two special debates were held. YouTube users
   sent in thousands of video questions, and a number were chosen as questions
   for candidates. The debate made people feel like an important part of the
15 election. **Suddenly**, thanks to YouTube, politics was cool again.

The site is also **changing the face of** news
reporting. In the Internet age, many people
are **losing trust in** information sources like
newspapers and TV news programs. At the
20 same time, there's a new group of reporters.
They are people like you and me, using **digital**
cameras to **record** events as they happen.

   More than anything, YouTube gives its members a voice. Every day,
   thousands of people use webcams and other cameras to record their opinions.
25 They talk, sing, play music, laugh, and cry.

   It's a worldwide movement, with more than half the videos coming from
   outside the USA. In the coming years, online video will likely become even
   more popular. As it does, YouTube hopes to remain the best place to watch it
   all happen.

   ³ sales channel – means of selling something
   ⁸ TV clip – small part of a TV program
   ¹² debate – discussion between people (who usually have different opinions)
   ¹⁴ candidate – person running for political office

Questions about the Reading Choose the best answer.

1. (　) What is the main idea?
   (A) It is easy to record a video with a digital camera.
   (B) Movie clips are one kind of video shown on YouTube.
   (C) Videos on YouTube are a popular way to communicate.
   (D) Young people like to feel important during elections.

2. (　) When was YouTube bought by another company?
   (A) 1990
   (B) 2005
   (C) 2006
   (D) 2008

3. (　) What was special about the YouTube debates?
   (A) People asked their questions via video.
   (B) Candidates had to answer some hard questions.
   (C) YouTube users watched the debates on TV.
   (D) News about the debates was posted on the Net.

4. (　) What does the word *programs* in line 19 mean?
   (A) packages
   (B) shows
   (C) schedules
   (D) courses

5. (　) Which of the following is NOT true?
   (A) Anybody with a digital camera can be an online reporter.
   (B) People sometimes cry in the videos that they upload.
   (C) Almost all the videos on YouTube come from the USA.
   (D) Google paid more than $1 billion for YouTube.

Writing about the Article Answer each question based on the article.

1. How many videos are watched on YouTube every day?
   More than _____.

2. How did the YouTube debates make people feel?
   They made people _____.

3. What is suggested about the future of online video?
   In the future, _____.

Vocabulary Building

Choose the best word to fill in each blank.

1. The weather can _____ people's moods. Many people get sad when it rains.
   (A) influence   (B) happen   (C) become   (D) watch

2. The _____ to choose a new president will be held next month.
   (A) election   (B) information   (C) question   (D) program

3. I was sleeping when, _____, there was a loud knock at the door.
   (A) likely   (B) easily   (C) suddenly   (D) partly

4. Some people say that you often change your mind. What's your _____ to that?
   (A) event   (B) voice   (C) power   (D) response

5. Writing is a good way to _____ your feelings. So is drawing.
   (A) laugh   (B) express   (C) choose   (D) happen

6. My wife and I both speak Korean, but we often _____ in English.
   (A) record   (B) influence   (C) become   (D) communicate

7. I _____ the whole wedding with my camera.
   (A) chose   (B) expected   (C) recorded   (D) opened

8. It's a(n) _____ recorder, so I can easily transfer videos to a computer.
   (A) important   (B) growing   (C) strong   (D) digital

Phrase Building

Write the correct phrase in each blank. (Remember to use the correct word form.)

● change the face of   ● send in   ● lose trust in   ● more than anything

Many people want to lose weight. However, they're _____ "quick loss" diet programs. Ken Michaels, an Australian doctor, is trying to _____ the diet industry. His method doesn't include pills or promises of fast weight loss. Instead, he teaches people about forming good habits. _____, Dr. Michaels says people should eat healthy, low-fat food. Exercise is the other key to good health and weight loss.

Grammar Exercise

Noun Clauses

Fill in each blank with *what*, *that*, **or** *where*.

Example: I don't know _____ the office is located.
Answer: I don't know *where* the office is located.

1. Do you know _____ the boss wants me to do with these files?

2. I learned _____ the house is 50 years old.

3. _____ he said about the case isn't important.

4. Let's find out _____ the nearest post office is.

5. We are certain _____ the other supplier can give us a better price.

Listening Exercise Track 50

Listen to the conversation. Then, answer the following questions.

1. (   ) In the video, where does the man jump up and down?
    (A) At home
    (B) At a restaurant
    (C) At work
    (D) At a college

2. (   ) What does Peter think might happen to the man in the video?
    (A) He could lose his job.
    (B) He may become famous on YouTube.
    (C) He might tell his boss.
    (D) He will show the video to a colleague.

3. (   ) What is the man told to do at the end of the video?
    (A) Jump up and down
    (B) Stop filming the video
    (C) Yell at someone else
    (D) Get down off the desk

Listening Activity   Track 51

Listen to the talk. Then, fill in the information in the chart.

1. What kind of products are they selling?	
2. How many ads do they already have?	
3. Where does he want to film students?	
4. Where will the company post the videos?	
5. What will be added to the videos?	

Discussion Questions

1. Many videos on YouTube are very personal. How would you feel about sharing your thoughts and feelings with everybody on the Internet?

2. Do you think the Internet is changing the world? If so, in what ways?

3. Many people get their news from blogs, personal videos, and other "non traditional" sources. What's good and bad about getting your news that way?

Discussion Activity

Working in groups of four, hold a mini YouTube debate. First, think of several questions to ask the candidates. Two students should ask the questions, and the other two should answer them. (Don't pretend to be a real politician. Just be yourself!) Some areas you might talk about are the environment, the economy, and education.

Example: A: If elected, what would you do to help the environment?
       B: First, I would encourage people to recycle more....

Discuss these questions in pairs.

1. Do you have any credit cards? If so, how many?

2. What are credit cards useful for?

3. Do you know anyone in serious credit card debt?

Consider the Topic

Read each statement. Check if you agree or disagree with it.

	agree	disagree
1. I often see TV and newspaper ads for credit cards.	☐	☐
2. It is easy to apply for new credit cards.	☐	☐
3. Credit card interest rates are very high.	☐	☐

Reading Passage

Track 52

1   Credit cards make life more convenient. They let us shop online, buy things over the phone, and pay for things easily. However, because of their high interest **rates**, using credit cards can be dangerous. For Taiwan's so-called "credit card slaves," that has led to serious **financial** problems.

5   In the early 2000s, credit cards and cash cards spread like wildfire in Taiwan. Banks **advertised** cards on TV, in newspapers, and on the Internet. They also set up booths all over the place to look for more customers. In just a few years, tens of millions of cards were issued.

     For those who paid off their card **balances** every month, things were fine.
10   However, with interest rates of 18-20%, those carrying large balances often **wound up** in a **cycle** of **debt**. In many cases, people had to use cash cards to **borrow** money to pay their bills. This made the cycle of debt even worse, since cash cards often have interest rates of 25%!

     People with a mountain of debt came to be known
15   as card slaves. By 2006, there were half a million people with 300,000 NT or more in debt. Many people were simply unable to pay their bills. That led to banks losing billions of dollars from unpaid loans. Clearly, something had to be done.

20   More than 200,000 people **worked out** repayment plans with banks. Plus, banks **cut back on** advertising credit cards and made it harder to apply for new ones. Also, a new law was passed in June 2007. It let people apply for bankruptcy if they could not work out a repayment plan.

     These moves helped reduce the problem. However, there are still thousands
25   of people with serious credit card debt. And, there are some 37 million credit cards and 2 million cash cards still in use. Hopefully, from the problem of credit card slaves, we've all learned a lesson about how to use (and not **abuse**) credit and cash cards.

---

3 interest rate – percentage charged on an unpaid credit card balance
16 NT – New Taiwan dollar (the currency of Taiwan)
20 repayment – returning something (often money); paying back
23 bankruptcy – the legal state of having no money at all

Questions about the Reading Choose the best answer.

1. (   ) What is the main idea?
   - (A) Credit cards, though convenient, can be a big problem.
   - (B) The interest rates for credit cards are very high.
   - (C) Internet shopping makes it easy to buy anything we want.
   - (D) People should only buy the things they need.

2. (   ) What led to the fast spread of credit cards and cash cards?
   - (A) Serious fires
   - (B) Credit card slaves
   - (C) Low interest rates
   - (D) Heavy advertising

3. (   ) How many "card slaves" were there in 2006?
   - (A) 200,000
   - (B) 300,000
   - (C) 500,000
   - (D) 2,000,000

4. (   ) Which credit card users got into trouble?
   - (A) People who had many bank accounts.
   - (B) People who applied for certain credit cards.
   - (C) People who used their cards every month.
   - (D) People who did not pay off large balances.

5. (   ) Which of the following is true?
   - (A) The average credit card interest rate is 25%.
   - (B) A law helping credit card slaves was passed in 2007.
   - (C) Most credit card users are 300,000 NT in debt.
   - (D) Cash card interest rates are lower than credit card rates.

Writing about the Article Answer each question based on the article.

1. Where did banks advertise credit cards?

   There were ads _____ .

2. How did banks suffer when many people stopped paying back loans?

   Banks lost _____ .

3. How many credit cards are still being used?

   There are _____ .

Vocabulary Building Choose the best word to fill in each blank.

1. As they say, the rich get richer, and the poor get poorer. It's a never-ending
_____.
   (A) rate   (B) cycle   (C) bill   (D) plan

2. Everyone I know has a lot of _____ – mostly from buying houses and cars.
   (A) payment   (B) debt   (C) cycle   (D) interest

3. My credit card _____ is still much higher than I would like it to be.
   (A) balance   (B) Internet   (C) customer   (D) booth

4. The company's _____ situation is good. They have plenty of cash.
   (A) major   (B) financial   (C) clear   (D) convenient

5. Can I _____ some money from you? I'm a few dollars short.
   (A) apply   (B) borrow   (C) repay   (D) work

6. Clothing companies love to _____ their products in magazines like *GQ*.
   (A) use   (B) lead   (C) reduce   (D) advertise

7. I'm afraid of using a credit card since the interest _____ is so high.
   (A) rate   (B) lesson   (C) online   (D) loan

8. Don't _____ your friend's kindness. Do something nice for him in return.
   (A) carry   (B) issue   (C) apply   (D) abuse

Phrase Building Write the correct phrase in each blank. (Remember to use the correct word form.)

● all over the place   ● work out   ● cut back on   ● wind up

Several years ago, Marcia went through a money crisis. She had several large debts, including home and car loans. Then, without warning, she lost her job. Immediately, she _____ eating out, shopping, and even talking on the phone. But it wasn't enough. Her debts were too big. So, Marcia went to a bank and _____ a way to get her debt under control. She _____ transferring all her credit card balances onto one card. Then, she cut up the rest of the cards.

Grammar Exercise

Adjectives vs. Adverbs

Choose the correct word to complete each sentence.

Example: Mei Ling is in (serious/seriously) debt.
Answer: Mei Ling is in (serious)/seriously) debt.

1. (Hopeful/Hopefully), we can finish in less than an hour.

2. I thought it was a very (sad/sadly) story.

3. It's (possible/possibly) that the event will be canceled.

4. The bicycle can (easy/easily) be repaired.

5. Mr. Drake is an (honest/honestly) man.

Listening Exercise   Track 53

Listen to the conversation. Then, answer the following questions.

1. (   ) What is the man's problem?
   (A) He cannot get a credit card.
   (B) He needs to borrow some money.
   (C) He should go to the doctor.
   (D) He has a large credit card balance.

2. (   ) What does the woman suggest doing?
   (A) Applying for another card
   (B) Talking to her friend
   (C) Cutting up his bills
   (D) Trying not to use the card

3. (   ) What is the man worried about?
   (A) Needing the card in the future
   (B) Doing something against the law
   (C) Paying the card off too quickly
   (D) Going somewhere very far away

Listening Activity 🔘 Track 54

Listen to the report. Then, fill in the information in the chart.

1. How many credit cards did Ms. Cheng use to have?	
2. What was her total debt in 2005?	
3. What percentage of her salary went towards paying credit card bills?	
4. Where did Ms. Cheng's friend work?	
5. How many credit cards does Ms. Cheng have now?	

Discussion Questions

1. Is there a "safe" way to use credit cards, or are they nothing but trouble?

2. What should be done when a person can't repay his or her credit card debt? Should the credit card company take the loss? Should the government pay? Should the person's relatives have to pay?

3. The main reason people get into credit card debt is because they shop too much. Is that a big problem in today's world? Do people want to buy too many things, even when they can't afford them?

Discussion Activity

Hold a mini debate about credit cards. On one side are two people with a positive view of credit cards. On the other side are two people who are strongly against the use of credit cards. Each side should spend a few minutes thinking of reasons for its point of view. Then, hold the mini debate.

Example: We think credit cards are very useful. The problem isn't with credit cards but with people who can't control themselves....

Discuss these questions in pairs.

1. How often do you exercise?

2. What kinds of exercise do you do?

3. Have you ever tried yoga?

Consider the Topic **Read each statement. Check if you agree or disagree with it.**

	agree	disagree
1. I have a lot of stress in my life.	☐	☐
2. There are places in my city to study yoga.	☐	☐
3. Some of my friends have tried yoga.	☐	☐

1   Many of us lead fast and busy lives. Computers and other tools make
     our lives easier, but we're still under a lot of **stress**. To help **cope with**
     the pressure, many people are turning to an **ancient** practice, yoga. It can
     improve health and lead to a **sense** of inner peace.

5   Yoga means "union." Its **goal** is to bring the body, mind, and spirit into
     harmony. The practice began in India a very long time ago. It was first
     written about more than 2,000 years ago in an important book, the *Bhagavad
     Gita*. Over time, many branches of yoga were **developed**. In modern India,
     the most popular branch is Bhakti Yoga. Like other types of yoga, it is
10   closely connected to the Hindu religion.

     Outside of India, many people, no matter what their religion is, have **taken**

up yoga. The Hatha style attracts people who want
to exercise. People sit and stand in different poses,
called "asanas." Some are very simple. Others take
15   years of study to master. In Hatha Yoga, attention
is also placed on **breathing** practices, called
"pranayama," and on meditation.

Yoga has a long list of benefits. It improves strength,
raises energy levels, and makes a person more
20   flexible. On top of that, yoga can help with problems
like back pain. And, it can help people lose **weight**.
What's more, yoga can lower one's stress level and
lead to a greater sense of calm.

     With all these benefits, it's no wonder there are yoga classes in so many
25   countries. Some new styles have even been developed outside of India.
     As we push into the 21st century, we will surely **discover** many incredible
     new things. It's interesting that we can still learn so much from an ancient
     practice like yoga.

---

6 harmony – order/peace
17 meditation – the practice of sitting quietly while clearing one's mind
20 flexible – easily bent, moved, or changed

Questions about the Reading   Choose the best answer.

1. (   ) What does yoga aim to do?
      (A) Get people to read the *Bhagavad Gita*
      (B) Help people make a lot of money
      (C) Teach people about India
      (D) Give people a feeling of harmony

2. (   ) What interests people in Hatha Yoga?
      (A) It can be used as a form of exercise.
      (B) It is the easiest style to teach.
      (C) Hatha is the oldest type of yoga.
      (D) The meditation style is quickly learned.

3. (   ) What is NOT a reason people practice yoga?
      (A) To become stronger
      (B) To become less flexible
      (C) To become less stressed
      (D) To become healthier

4. (   ) What does the phrase *on top of* in line 20 mean?
      (A) in spite of
      (B) in exchange for
      (C) in addition to
      (D) in place of

5. (   ) Which of the following is true?
      (A) All styles of yoga are thousands of years old.
      (B) Many people in India practice Bhakti Yoga.
      (C) Every style of yoga was developed in India.
      (D) Pranayama is another word for "meditation."

Writing about the Article   Answer each question based on the article.

1. When was the *Bhagavad Gita* written?

   It was _____ .

2. What religion is yoga closely connected to?

   It is closely _____ .

3. What is an asana?

   An asana is _____ .

Vocabulary Building   Choose the best word to fill in each blank.

1. It's a(n) _____ building. It has been here for more than 1,500 years.
   (A) ancient   (B) important   (C) simple   (D) interested

2. Our _____ is to open three new stores this year.
   (A) type   (B) calm   (C) goal   (D) yoga

3. We _____ this pool while hiking here last month. It's a great place to swim.
   (A) improved   (B) discovered   (C) practiced   (D) developed

4. When I talked to John, I got the _____ that something was wrong.
   (A) branch   (B) style   (C) sense   (D) body

5. Bus drivers have a lot of _____. That's not surprising, since traffic is often very bad.
   (A) stress   (B) energy   (C) peace   (D) study

6. If you want to lose _____, start by eating less candy.
   (A) weight   (B) religion   (C) exercise   (D) benefit

7. In outer space and underwater, people need special equipment to _____.
   (A) discover   (B) lower   (C) improve   (D) breathe

8. It will take the car company four years to _____ a new model.
   (A) develop   (B) raise   (C) stand   (D) place

Phrase Building   Write the correct phrase in each blank. (Remember to use the correct word form.)

● take up   ● cope with   ● what's more   ● lead to

Patty is having a hard time _____ all her responsibilities. She works full-time and takes care of her mother. _____, she watches her brother's children three days a week. Sometimes, her life can be very stressful. Patty's best friend thinks she should join a spa or _____ yoga. Patty is thinking it over. Though she doesn't mind doing so much for others, it would be nice to have a few hours a week to herself.

Grammar Exercise

Singular vs. Plural

Choose the correct answer.

Example: One of my best friends (lives/live) in Kenya.
Answer: One of my best friends (lives)/live) in Kenya.

1. All the people here (has/have) had two years of training.

2. Several of the children (is/are) playing volleyball.

3. The person who usually delivers my packages (was/were) sick yesterday.

4. The price of a bottle of milk (has/have) gone up recently.

5. Every set meal on the menu (comes/come) with a drink and dessert.

Listening Exercise   Track 56

Listen to the conversation. Then, answer the following questions.

1. (   ) What does the woman invite the man to do?
    (A) Teach her yoga
    (B) Go on a trip
    (C) Take some photos
    (D) Attend a class

2. (   ) What worries the man?
    (A) Practicing yoga will hurt.
    (B) His friend is overweight.
    (C) The class will be expensive.
    (D) He is already in pain.

3. (   ) What does the woman imply?
    (A) Not all students of yoga are thin.
    (B) At first, learning yoga may be difficult.
    (C) When practicing yoga, it helps to be tall.
    (D) She has studied yoga for years.

Listening Activity   Track 57

Listen to the advertisement. Then, fill in the information in the chart.

1. What is the name of the school?	
2. When did it open?	
3. How much experience do the teachers have?	
4. What time do evening classes start?	
5. How can people get more information?	

Discussion Questions

1. In your country, is yoga practiced more by men or women, or is it about the same? If there is a difference, why do you think that is?

2. Many people (especially in cities) lead stressful lives. What are the sources of that stress?

3. In our busy world, some people are looking for a calmer and more peaceful life. Others enjoy the excitement and fast pace. How about you?

Discussion Activity

Your company wants everyone to get into better shape. Develop a plan to make your colleagues healthier. That includes physical and mental health. You might consider an exercise plan. Also, think about ways for employees to eat better. Plus, are there any changes you could make to the workplace environment?

Example: First, we want to make the office more comfortable. Some plants would help with that. Also, a relaxing break room would be a good idea....

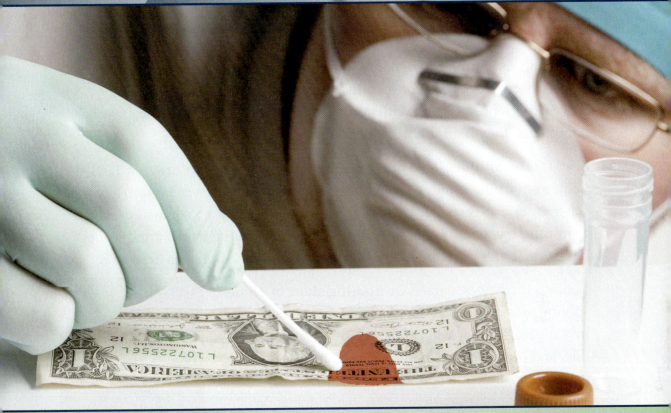

Pre-Reading Questions · Discuss these questions in pairs.

1. What kinds of crimes are often reported on in the news?

2. Have you ever watched the TV show *CSI*?

3. What kinds of evidence are collected at a crime scene? (Ex: blood)

Consider the Topic · Read each statement. Check if you agree or disagree with it.

	agree	disagree
1. TV shows about police work are interesting.	☐	☐
2. Scientists who work for the police have exciting jobs.	☐	☐
3. Technology is an important part of scientists' work.	☐	☐

Reading Passage   ⊙ Track 58

1   **Criminals** are finding it harder to hide from the law. That's because they're **up against** a special type of **scientist**. Trained with the latest technology, "forensic scientists" work with police departments. Using microscopes and computers, they help **solve** even the most difficult cases.

5   Scientific **techniques** have been used in police work for centuries. In 1248, a book from China listed ways to figure out what weapon was used in a crime. Later, in 1775, a Swedish scientist learned how to tell if poison was used to murder someone. Then, in 1835, police officers in England started using ballistics. It's a technique to match a bullet with the gun it was fired from.

10   Today's forensic scientists are **nothing short of** crime solving masters. **On the front lines** are crime scene investigators. They collect fingerprints, blood, hair, dirt, and other items at crime scenes. This type of work has been made famous by TV shows like *CSI*.

15   The shows don't **exactly match** the working style of real scientists. However, some of it is similar.

Back at the lab, items from a crime scene are studied. Using a comparison microscope, scientists can check if a hair sample matches a suspect's hair. DNA taken

20   from a drop of blood can also be fed into a computer. The sample is compared to the information in a database. If there's a match, it's evidence that a suspect was at the scene. It may be enough to **prove** that he or she committed a crime.

To carry out these difficult jobs, forensic scientists need to be highly skilled. They often have degrees in biology or chemistry. Many also have **knowledge**

25   of police work. Their work isn't always as exciting as that shown on *CSI*. However, it's still very important. These crime fighters in white lab coats help police officers catch more criminals. That makes our cities and streets safer.

---

³ microscope – machine that makes things look larger
⁶ weapon – something used to hurt someone (like a gun)
⁸ murder – kill
¹² investigator – person who examines and researches something (like a crime)
¹⁹ suspect – someone who may have done something (like commit a murder)
²¹ database – collection of information
²² commit – do/perform

Questions about the Reading   Choose the best answer.

1. (   ) What is the main idea?
      (A) *CSI* is a great television show.
      (B) Computers are important in many fields.
      (C) Criminals are smarter than ever.
      (D) Scientists often help the police solve crimes.

2. (   ) When did a European scientist learn how to tell if someone was poisoned?
      (A) 1248
      (B) 1775
      (C) 1835
      (D) 2008

3. (   ) What does the article suggest about real crime scene investigators?
      (A) Their work is the same as that shown on *CSI*.
      (B) Only a few know a lot about police work.
      (C) They collect very important evidence.
      (D) Once in a while, they get jobs on TV shows.

4. (   ) What do scientists do with a comparison microscope?
      (A) They feed information into a computer.
      (B) They read the information in a database.
      (C) They create evidence for a crime scene.
      (D) They look at two of the same types of items.

5. (   ) Which of the following is true?
      (A) Every forensic scientist has a chemistry degree.
      (B) Ballistics are used to compare blood samples.
      (C) DNA evidence can prove who committed a crime.
      (D) Scientists first started helping the police 100 years ago.

Writing about the Article   Answer each question based on the article.

1. When was ballistics first used in police work?

   Police officers first _____ .

2. At a lab, what is blood from a crime scene compared to?

   It is compared to _____ .

3. What degrees do forensic scientists often have?

   They often _____ .

117

Vocabulary Building   Choose the best word to fill in each blank.

1. It's _____ the right size for my living room. I'll take it.
   (A) excitingly   (B) hardly   (C) exactly   (D) highly

2. I can _____ that the purse is mine. It has my driver's license in it.
   (A) prove   (B) catch   (C) compare   (D) solve

3. My mother taught me a great _____ for growing beautiful roses.
   (A) sample   (B) technique   (C) scene   (D) biology

4. Some bones were found in the park. _____ are trying to figure out
   where they came from.
   (A) Scientists   (B) Crimes   (C) Degrees   (D) Microscopes

5. After we _____ the power problem, we were able to produce very small
   computers.
   (A) trained   (B) collected   (C) solved   (D) matched

6. Mr. Lennon is full of _____ about New Zealand's history.
   (A) knowledge   (B) blood   (C) law   (D) style

7. The police caught the _____ after chasing him for three hours.
   (A) evidence   (B) criminal   (C) style   (D) fingerprint

8. We can use this program to _____ a photo with a person's name.
   (A) match   (B) prove   (C) feed   (D) train

Phrase Building   Write the correct phrase in each blank.

● nothing short of   ● up against   ● on the front lines   ● figure out

Lydia is _____ a genius. She's a computer master and a security expert. And, she's _____ of the banking industry's fight against theft. Now, Lydia is developing a new kind of video camera. If she's successful, the camera will know when a crime is in progress. A message will then be secretly sent to the police. Lydia knows she's _____ a big challenge, but it's an important task. The new system will help protect a bank, its employees, and its customers.

Grammar Exercise

Be, Been, and Being

Fill in each blank with *be,* *been,* **or** *being.*

Example: We have _____ loyal customers for 12 years.
Answer: We have *been* loyal customers for 12 years.

1. The neighbors are _____ loud. Can you ask them to quiet down?

2. The store is expensive, but it may _____ the only place that sells the equipment we need.

3. I love _____ a teacher. It's work that I can feel good about.

4. Has Ed _____ in India for 20 years? I didn't know that.

5. I'd like to _____ the project leader, if you don't mind.

Listening Exercise   Track 59

Listen to the conversation. Then, answer the following questions.

1. (   ) How long was the Canadian man in jail?
  (A) 4 years
  (B) 10 years
  (C) 14 years
  (D) 40 years

2. (   ) What led to the man being freed?
  (A) A DNA comparison
  (B) A new crime scene photo
  (C) A request from the victim
  (D) A jail being closed

3. (   ) What does the woman suggest about the case?
  (A) It is not the only case of its kind.
  (B) It is proof that nobody should be in jail.
  (C) It is a sign that crime rates are falling.
  (D) It is different from one she heard about.

Listening Activity   Track 60

Listen to the report. Then, fill in the information in the chart.

1. What is becoming harder to do?	
2. What are police calling this problem?	
3. What is often used to solve cases on TV?	
4. What is true about many real world crime scenes?	
5. When do criminal lawyers bring up this fact?	

Discussion Questions

1. Newspapers and TV programs love to report on crimes. Do you feel like your country is becoming more dangerous or less dangerous? Or, is it about the same as before?

2. Actors on TV shows like *CSI* often solve crimes within days. Real police officers say that's not realistic. Do you think TV shows should be realistic, or is it unnecessary?

3. Some governments want to collect samples of every person's DNA. They say it will help catch criminals. Is that a good or bad idea? Why?

Discussion Activity

You and several classmates are crime scene investigators. Last night, a body was found in front of a bar. You have to figure out who committed the murder. First, make a list of the kinds of evidence you will look for. Then, make up a story about how you solved the crime.

Example: At the crime scene, we collected blood and hair samples. We also found several pieces of glass....

Target Word List

☐ abroad	Unit 15	☐ damage	Unit 9
☐ abuse	Unit 18	☐ deadline	Unit 8
☐ admire	Unit 11	☐ deal	Unit 6
☐ advertise	Unit 18	☐ debt	Unit 18
☐ affect	Unit 14	☐ deliver	Unit 4
☐ alike	Unit 10	☐ demand	Unit 2
☐ ancient	Unit 19	☐ deserve	Unit 3
☐ announce	Unit 11	☐ develop	Unit 19
☐ artistic	Unit 8	☐ device	Unit 1
☐ attend	Unit 13	☐ digital	Unit 17
☐ average	Unit 16	☐ discover	Unit 19
☐ background	Unit 13	☐ disease	Unit 11
☐ balance	Unit 18	☐ domestic	Unit 10
☐ blame	Unit 7	☐ donate	Unit 11
☐ borrow	Unit 18	☐ effect	Unit 5
☐ brand	Unit 10	☐ election	Unit 17
☐ breathe	Unit 19	☐ encourage	Unit 16
☐ career	Unit 7	☐ entirely	Unit 12
☐ character	Unit 12	☐ environment	Unit 2
☐ charity	Unit 11	☐ equipment	Unit 8
☐ client	Unit 8	☐ exactly	Unit 20
☐ communicate	Unit 17	☐ exhibition	Unit 6
☐ constant	Unit 7	☐ export	Unit 15
☐ consumer	Unit 2	☐ express	Unit 17
☐ criminal	Unit 20	☐ fake	Unit 12
☐ crisis	Unit 14	☐ fancy	Unit 3
☐ curious	Unit 7	☐ fashion	Unit 4
☐ custom	Unit 15	☐ financial	Unit 18
☐ cycle	Unit 18	☐ firm	Unit 4

☐ focus	Unit 10		☐ likewise	Unit 15
☐ following	Unit 12		☐ limited	Unit 14
☐ force	Unit 5		☐ luxury	Unit 3
☐ forest	Unit 9		☐ match	Unit 20
☐ friendship	Unit 3		☐ media	Unit 7
☐ function	Unit 1		☐ mix	Unit 10
☐ generally	Unit 2		☐ monitor	Unit 9
☐ global	Unit 6		☐ movement	Unit 12
☐ goal	Unit 19		☐ neighborhood	Unit 13
☐ gorgeous	Unit 3		☐ network	Unit 8
☐ gossip	Unit 7		☐ non-profit	Unit 1
☐ greet	Unit 13		☐ nutrition	Unit 16
☐ happen	Unit 8		☐ oil	Unit 2
☐ harm	Unit 15		☐ option	Unit 11
☐ health	Unit 14		☐ outfit	Unit 4
☐ ideally	Unit 9		☐ personality	Unit 13
☐ ignore	Unit 7		☐ pet	Unit 3
☐ image	Unit 8		☐ popular	Unit 6
☐ imagination	Unit 12		☐ powerful	Unit 1
☐ imagine	Unit 10		☐ prefer	Unit 2
☐ impossible	Unit 7		☐ prepare	Unit 10
☐ influence	Unit 17		☐ process	Unit 12
☐ international	Unit 13		☐ promote	Unit 4
☐ invention	Unit 10		☐ proud	Unit 13
☐ issue	Unit 16		☐ prove	Unit 20
☐ item	Unit 6		☐ provide	Unit 3
☐ knowledge	Unit 20		☐ rapid	Unit 15
☐ launch	Unit 5		☐ rate	Unit 18
☐ leader	Unit 1		☐ rather	Unit 12

☐ reach	Unit 16		☐ tiny	Unit 4
☐ record	Unit 17		☐ translate	Unit 15
☐ reputation	Unit 4		☐ trend	Unit 11
☐ require	Unit 3		☐ unfortunately	Unit 5
☐ response	Unit 17		☐ unhealthy	Unit 15
☐ retire	Unit 16		☐ useful	Unit 5
☐ revenue	Unit 6		☐ valuable	Unit 6
☐ reverse	Unit 9		☐ variety	Unit 13
☐ scholar	Unit 1		☐ vary	Unit 8
☐ scientist	Unit 20		☐ waste	Unit 14
☐ sense	Unit 19		☐ waterproof	Unit 1
☐ setback	Unit 9		☐ wealthy	Unit 11
☐ severe	Unit 9		☐ wedding	Unit 4
☐ share	Unit 5		☐ weight	Unit 19
☐ sharply	Unit 14		☐ withstand	Unit 1
☐ similar	Unit 16			
☐ situation	Unit 14			
☐ solve	Unit 20			
☐ species	Unit 9			
☐ speed	Unit 2			
☐ spread	Unit 5			
☐ stable	Unit 16			
☐ strategy	Unit 5			
☐ stress	Unit 19			
☐ suddenly	Unit 17			
☐ superstar	Unit 6			
☐ supply	Unit 14			
☐ target	Unit 2			
☐ technique	Unit 20			

Target Phrase List

☐ a bite to eat	Unit 3		☐ make one's way	Unit 15
☐ a whole host of	Unit 2		☐ make room for	Unit 9
☐ all the time	Unit 2		☐ meet up	Unit 15
☐ as far back as	Unit 12		☐ more than anything	Unit 17
☐ as many as	Unit 14		☐ move away from	Unit 2
☐ at the end of the day	Unit 7		☐ nothing short of	Unit 20
☐ aware of	Unit 4		☐ on the front lines	Unit 20
☐ branch into	Unit 4		☐ on the go	Unit 10
☐ can't bear to	Unit 3		☐ on the lookout	Unit 5
☐ cause for alarm	Unit 9		☐ on top of	Unit 6
☐ change the face of	Unit 17		☐ one by one	Unit 12
☐ come across	Unit 5		☐ out of work	Unit 12
☐ cope with	Unit 19		☐ out on the town	Unit 3
☐ cut back on	Unit 18		☐ put pressure on	Unit 14
☐ do the trick	Unit 8		☐ regardless of	Unit 7
☐ due to	Unit 16		☐ rely on	Unit 14
☐ earn a living	Unit 8		☐ spread out	Unit 13
☐ fall on	Unit 16		☐ stand out	Unit 10
☐ far from	Unit 6		☐ take off	Unit 4
☐ get around	Unit 13		☐ take on	Unit 6
☐ give away	Unit 11		☐ take steps	Unit 9
☐ go into production	Unit 1		☐ take up	Unit 19
☐ hold onto	Unit 11		☐ think up	Unit 5
☐ in a rush	Unit 16		☐ turn around	Unit 11
☐ in no time	Unit 15		☐ turn out	Unit 1
☐ in that	Unit 1		☐ up against	Unit 20
☐ in the face of	Unit 10		☐ what's more	Unit 19
☐ in the public eye	Unit 7		☐ wind up	Unit 18
☐ lose trust in	Unit 17		☐ word of mouth	Unit 8
☐ made up of	Unit 13		☐ work out	Unit 18

About the Author

Andrew E. Bennett holds an EdM (Master of Education) degree from Harvard University and a BA degree from UC Santa Cruz. He has studied seven languages. It's a life-long passion that began with a study of Spanish and continues with his ongoing studies of Chinese and Japanese.

Andrew has been involved in English education since 1993, both as a teacher and a writer. He has taught a variety of subjects, including English composition, business writing, English literature, and TOEFL preparation.

Andrew is the author of more than 30 English learning books, including classroom texts, supplementary books, self-study books, as well as TOEIC preparation texts. In addition to writing and teaching, he regularly attends ESL conferences and gives presentations to groups of teachers at schools and symposiums.

Central to Andrew's teaching philosophy is an emphasis on content. His work includes subjects from countries around the world, giving his writing an international flavor. Andrew also enjoys writing about cultural issues, as he is convinced of the vital link between language and culture.